Cycle touring in Europe

Frontispiece: In the Quantock Hills, Somerset

Constable London

Cycle touring in Europe
Peter Knottley

First published in Great Britain 1975
by Constable and Company Ltd
10 Orange Street London WC2H 7EG
Copyright © 1975 Peter Knottley

ISBN 0 09 460840 7

Set in Monophoto Apollo
Filmset and printed in Great Britain by
BAS Printers Limited, Wallop, Hampshire

Contents

Introduction   10

1   **The bicycle**   13
Choosing one. Its parts, their maintenance and
adjustment. How to ride. Tandems. Tricycles.
Family cycling. A note for the ladies.

2   **Before the tour**   38
Riding experience. Checking the cycle.

3   **Taking the bicycle for a ride**   42

4   **What to take**   47
Clothing. Spares and tools.

5   **How to take it**   56

6   **Maps**   61

7   **On tour**   67
Distance. Food. Accommodation.

8   **Cycle-camping**   75

9   **Touring in Europe**   82
Passports. Visas. Currency. Customs. Health.
Language. Cycling and travel.

10   **The countries of Europe**   94
Getting to them. Travelling and cycling in them.
Accommodation. Some touring areas. Climate.
Language. Maps.
Austria – Belgium and Luxembourg – Bulgaria –

Cyprus – Czechoslovakia – Denmark – Finland –
France – Germany (East and West) – Greece –
Hungary – Iceland – Irish Republic – Italy – Malta –
Netherlands – Norway – Poland – Portugal –
Rumania – Spain – Sweden – Switzerland –
Turkey-in-Europe – United Kingdom (England,
Scotland, Wales, Northern Ireland) – Yugoslavia.

11 **What it's really like**   196
    Cycle-camping in Scotland. In the Pyrenees. Ten in
    Somerset.

12 **Some suggested cycling tours**   222
    Wessex. The Cotswolds. Wales. Suffolk and Norfolk.
    Yorkshire Dales and Moors. France. Austria and
    Germany.

    Equipment lists   237
    Official National Tourist Offices in London.   240
    Useful addresses and publications.   242
    Metric conversion tables.   245
    Time differences in European countries.   246
    Units of currency   248
    Average monthly temperatures of selected   249
    European towns.

    Index   251

Illustrations

Frontispiece: In the Quantock Hills, Somerset

Go to a specialist cycle dealer . . .
Who offers good after-sales service   14

The anatomy of the bicycle   16

There is a variety of comfortable positions for the
hands on dropped handlebars   21

Gear mechanisms   26

Family cycling   34/5

All youngsters want a bicycle   36

To Australia by Moulton bicycle   48

Carrier for front pannier bags   57

Touring cycle complete with saddlebag, front and
rear panniers and handlebar bag   59

Maps   64/5

A group of cycle tourists leaving Bellingham youth
hostel, Northumberland   72

A party of cycle-campers from the USA at a site on
the Thames   76

The simplicity and freedom of cycle-camping   78

A keen cyclist will take his cycle everywhere!   83

Towpath cycling takes one along very pleasant and
unfrequented ways   92

Most of Europe has a network of minor roads
which are ideal for cycle tourists   118

Summer sunshine   120

At the Black Lake, near the start of the crossing of
the Gap of Dunloe in Killarney, Ireland   140

Fording the stream   150

Cyclists enjoying a New Year's Day run in Surrey   180

Near the Scottish border there is plenty of open
country with quiet roads   184

A section of the crowd attending a cycle touring
rally in Surrey   194

Some cycle tourists are determined to reach the top 219

An expedition group off the beaten track in the
hills of North Wales   227

Cycle visitors to Europe from the United States   229

Winter sunshine   235

Puncture!   239

Acknowledgements

If this book helps the reader to share in some measure the delight which I find in cycle touring, we shall both be content.

My thanks go to Leslie Warner, national secretary of the Cyclists' Touring Club, and his wife Sheila, for reading some of the material and making useful comments, to Geoffrey Stumm, manager of C.T.C. Travel Ltd., and to several other cycle tourists who have willingly helped on specific points.

Introduction

Cycle touring is fun. Easy, simple fun, which is equally enjoyed by young and old, by the physically strong and the not so strong. A great advantage of cycling is that it is an exercise which is rhythmic and beneficial but not strenuous and it can be undertaken by people of all ages and all sorts and conditions with very few exceptions.

Cycle touring is a great deal more than just good exercise though. There is far more to it than just travelling. It is perhaps the only really independent means of getting about; stopping and starting at will, you can have a carefree journey which is every bit as important and satisfying as the arrival.

You meet the people when cycling – and they are glad to meet you. There is an interest and respect shown to cyclists which is not extended to other travellers, more so abroad than in Britain, although here too the envious glances are obvious as one moves smoothly by.

Instead of catching the occasional glimpse of fine scenery, the cyclist sees the panorama unfolding as he goes along. Instead of passing castles, historic buildings, scenes worthy of a photograph and all the many fascinations of his own country and others, he can stop and appreciate his fancies fully. Instead of the occasional encounter with local people, he becomes one of them, and can know what many have forgotten and many more perhaps did not know existed – a relaxed and friendly way of life which goes on in full measure in every country once you are off the busy highways.

In Europe, which this book is about, there is a vast

network of little-used roads awaiting the cyclist. Britain is particularly lucky in this respect; the touring cyclist will rarely be seen on a main road but finds his way with a little consultation of the map, using lanes and minor roads all the time. He discovers hamlets and topographical features of all kinds which are hidden from the mere 'traveller'. The same can be said of most of the mainland of Europe.

It is the sheer pleasure to be derived from touring by cycle which makes nearly all those who once taste its joys keep on doing it. That it is an education in itself, one of the best means to health, and cheap, are incidental, but real advantages.

There are some 'package tours' for cyclists on offer at home and abroad each year, at prices which compare very favourably with other modes of travel which usually go by this name. If you are new to cycle touring, it might be a good idea to try one of them for a start – lots do, but before long they discover how easy it is to plan your own tailor-made trip and to carry it out. It is then that you find that fine food and accommodation are available almost everywhere far more economically than is popularly supposed – and you will realise that all cyclists are quite fussy about their food and sleep. Quality and sufficiency of both are essential.

Truly the world is at the cyclist's feet. Louise Sutherland, a New Zealand lass, has already cycled 30,000 miles in 53 countries and is far from the end of her adventures. Cycling round the world – surely the ultimate in tours – has been going on ever since bicycles were invented, and that's nearly a century.

You don't have to be as ambitious as that, but it would be surprising if the urge to explore were completely absent from your make-up. Certainly, too, within a 25 mile radius of your home there are sights and sounds and a great deal of interest that you quite probably don't know exist but which you can so readily discover by means of the simple bicycle.

I hope, however, that you will get a little further than that, and that this book will help you to do so.

1

The bicycle

Choosing one
It is a big mistake, but a common one, to think that all cycles are alike and that 'any old bike' will do for you. Bicycles are individual things – like clothes, you can use various shapes and sizes within limits, but only those of the correct style and measurements will look, and be, comfortable. The quickest way to be persuaded that cycling is not for you is to use an unsuitable machine. But care in the selection and adjustment of the cycle will at once demonstrate the easy pleasure of cycling, and its comfort and safety.

Also like clothes, bicycles may be bought 'off the peg' or 'made to measure'. A wide variety of standard machines is available for all kinds of riding and they are capable of adjustment to suit individuals. Specially built frames, equipped with accessories of their own choice, are favoured by those who ride regularly, experience having shown them exactly what their needs and preferences are. These will cost more but will be properly 'tailored' to fit by a bespoke builder.

Buy the best you can afford for the purpose you have in mind; all modern cycles will give many thousands of miles of good service with just the essential maintenance and replacement of wearing parts such as tyres, brake blocks, cables etc.

Obtain your cycle from a specialist dealer who will be able to give you detailed advice, and who will not let the machine leave his premises unless it is in first-class order for the road.

Go to a specialist cycle dealer . . .   Who offers good after-sales service

The shop which handles cycles as a sideline, or a mail order store, will not be able to offer the advice nor give the expert check-over before handing the machine over to you – and there will be no after-sales service.

Its parts, their maintenance and adjustment
Let us look at all the bits and pieces which go to make up a bicycle, and consider their features together with their upkeep and adjustment.

Frame
The crucial item. Be fastidious in your choice of size and shape. Conventionally, the frame 'size' is the length of the seat tube – from its top down to the centre-line of the bottom bracket spindle. It varies from 15″ for children to 18″/20″ for people of small physique and up to 24″ or even more for tall people. Frames are normally available in 1″ steps (though in-between sizes can be made to order), and it is between 21″ and 23″ that most people find their suitable frame size. A good rule-of-thumb method for working out your size is to take the inside leg measurement and deduct 8″ from it. Try that size first, making sure that, with your hands resting lightly on the handlebars, you are able to sit on the saddle comfortably with the ball of one foot on the ground and the other foot on the pedal. Minor adjustments can be made by raising or lowering the saddle or the handlebars or both.

The shape of the conventional ('diamond' or 'triangle') frame is determined by two angles; one formed by the top tube (crossbar) and the handlebar stem, the second by the other end of the top tube and the seat tube.

The popular angles are 72°/72°, giving parallel front and seat tubes. This design affords responsiveness and a comfortable riding position with a wheelbase long enough for stability but short enough for liveliness.

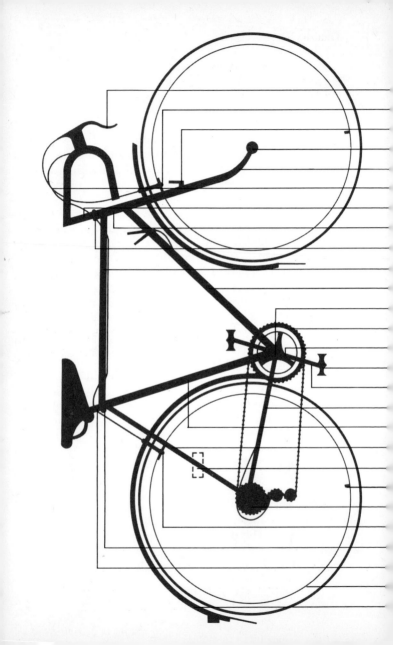

Brake Lever

Brake Shoes & Blocks

Lamp Bracket

Front Hub

Front Forks

Brake Cable

Handlebar Stem

Head

Lock Nut for Head & Handlebar Stem

Top Tube

Down Tube

Bottom Bracket Assembly

Chainwheel(s)

Cotter Pin or fixing bolt for cotterless crank

Pedal

Crank

Chain Stays

Seat Tube

Seat Stays

Rear Lamp

Valve

Cog(s) and Freewheel or single cog fixed wheel

Brake Shoes & Blocks

Adjusting Nut for Saddle Height

Seat Pillar

Rim

Rear Mudguard

Frames for ladies traditionally have the open design in which the upper tube slopes downwards to parallel the down tube, but for regular cycling the ladies now normally choose the 'man's' design for greater strength and steadiness.

Many varieties of small-wheel cycles are available. Most of them, though suitable for local and 'utility' riding, are inappropriate for long-distance work from the point of view of both riding comfort and load-carrying capacity. The exception is the Moulton bicycle, which, with its unique and scientific design – particularly the suspension system for the rear wheel – offers a most comfortable ride, and whose frames for carrying bags front and rear not only provide good bag capacity for all one's kit, but use bags which are very convenient for handling when not on the cycle.

Unfortunately the Moulton is in short supply, but it is hoped that new models will be in production before long. They are worth looking out for. They are unisex machines.

Bottom bracket

At the junction of seat tube, down tube and rear wheel stays, this houses the axle carrying the chainwheel and pedal cranks. Ball bearings $\frac{1}{4}''$ in diameter run at each end between precision machined faces on the axle and outer cups, packed with thick water-repellent grease. Adjustment is by means of a threaded removable cap on the near side, secured by a locking ring such that the axle rotates freely but without lateral or vertical movement at the ends. A little lubrication with thin oil every six months is enough here. The bearings should last for at least 5,000 miles; any broken ball bearing will not only make itself heard but will also make itself felt through the cranks when pedalling. Immediate replacement should be

made before more bearings are affected; replacement of
the whole set is in any case advisable.

The height above ground of the bracket varies – about
11" is usually right. Too high a bottom bracket will cause
discomfort and if it is too low it will possibly cause the
pedal to touch the ground when cornering.

Cranks and pedals

Cranks are made from steel (with cotter-pin fixing to the
bottom bracket axle) or alloy (cotterless, an almost square
axle end matching a slot in the crank which is secured by
a special bolt, needing a special tool for fixing and
dismantling). They are not interchangeable, requiring
different designs of axle. There is little to choose between
them though the cotterless is perhaps marginally more
efficient. Remember too that the more alloy components
used – although more expensive – the greater the overall
saving in weight.

Crank length can vary a little. It is normally $6\frac{1}{2}$"–7",
but is usually matched by the cycle builder to the
bottom bracket height.

Pedals come with rubber treads or with serrated metal
treads; the latter are the universal choice of tourists as
they are much more durable than rubber. Feet may slip
on either type, but toe-clips can be attached to metal
pedals. Toe-clips are widely favoured not only to prevent
slipping but also to locate the foot in the right position on
the pedal all the time. Both features make for the best
return for energy expended. Fairly frequent lubrication
of the bearings at the crank end of the pedal spindle is
recommended. They get much wear and of all the
bearings on a bicycle are the most exposed.

Handlebars

Flat, slightly raised or dropped? Flat or raised bars give a

comfortable position, but the advantage of the
generally-favoured dropped handlebar is that it gives
several different positions for the hands when riding. A
change of position now and again is pleasant and reduces
the possibility of fatigue; also, certain positions are
appropriate to certain conditions. Gripping the bars at the
top is advantageous when climbing because in that way
better use is made of the power of the muscles of the
back.

Holding the bars 'on the drops', or at the bottom, is the
least used position of the tourist although in a headwind
it reduces the area of the body exposed to the wind and
is very helpful 'streamlining'. The normal grip is with the
hands over the brake lever hoods, with an occasional
move to the upper bend of the bars simply for a change.
Any type of handlebar may be fitted to any cycle. The
average width of the handlebars is 15", but a large person
will need them an inch or two wider. Steering should be
free and easy. Any stiffness is readily apparent, and the
slightest vibration through the frame when applying the
front brake indicates looseness in the headset.
Adjustment is made by loosening the locknut at the top
of the headset, tightening or loosening the headnut and
tightening the locknut again.

To raise or lower the handlebars the expander bolt is
loosened – this is the bolt whose head tightens on to the
top of the handlebar stem. Tap the bolt head to free the
expander cone inside the stem, and the stem may be
moved up or down to the desired position, after which
the bolt is tightened again. There must be at least $2\frac{1}{2}''$ of
handlebar stem in the cycle tube. (Some handlebar stems
have Allen-key type expander bolts. A special spanner or

There is a variety of comfortable positions for the hands on
dropped handlebars

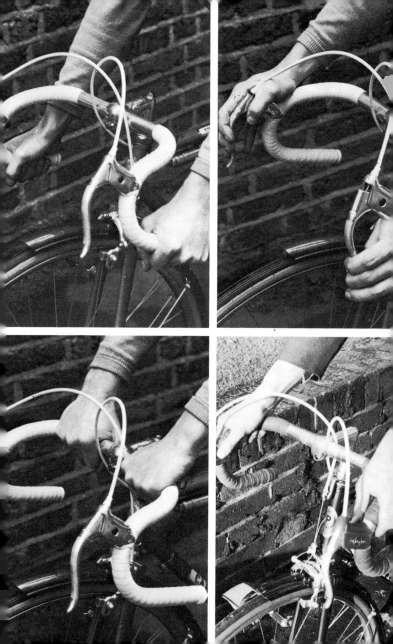

'key' is required for these, otherwise the procedure is the same.)

The handlebar angle is readily adjusted by loosening the nut on the centre clamp. As a rough guide, an acceptable angle for dropped handlebars is made when they are adjusted so that the ends of the bars point towards the hub of the rear wheel.

Saddle

This item is always very close to you and must be chosen with care. The cushion type saddle, with metal frame and felt top, suspended on springs and fabric-covered, may be all right for short rides, but not for longer touring when it gets uncomfortably hot – and it will not last long before fraying.

Leather saddles remain the most popular, being very hard-wearing and long-lasting, and it does not take long to get accustomed to them. Occasional treatment with 'Proofide' or dubbin will keep them supple. Plastic saddles are gaining in esteem, largely because they are now cheaper, but they do not 'breathe' and 'give' in the unique way which leather does. Plastic saddles covered with thin, soft leather are also made; they are good but wear and fray in due course.

It is a question of personal preference again, but whichever type of saddle you choose, be quite sure that it is wide enough to support the bones of the pelvis. Otherwise you will think that you are sitting on a beer bottle and will suffer severely.

The saddle is bolted to the 'seat pillar', the other end of which is clamped into the seat tube of the frame. The height of the saddle may be adjusted within narrow limits by altering the amount of seat pillar entering the frame (again, there should always be at least $2\frac{1}{2}''$ of pillar in the frame); it should project from the frame by

between 2″ and 4″ and outside these limits a wrong
frame size is indicated. The metal chassis of the saddle has
nuts and bolts giving adjustments to the angle of slope of
the saddle – horizontal or very slightly raised forward
will be found best – and 'fore-and-aft' adjustment.

Brakes
These will be of the calliper flexible wire type, made
with side-pull or centre-pull mechanism. The latter are
superior as they alone ensure an even application of both
brake blocks to the wheel rim when the levers are
pulled. There are side-pull brakes available which are
quite satisfactory but their design inherently inhibits the
same action; the pressure on both brake blocks cannot be
quite equalised. Rod operated brakes are not suitable for
touring cycles.

   Brakes should be adjusted so that the brake blocks are
held about $\frac{1}{16}$″ away from the rims. All cable brakes are
capable of adjustment by loosening the cable clamp at the
brake end, pulling the cable through to the correct
position and tightening up again. Some makes of brake
have a built-in adjuster which avoids this procedure for
minor alterations to the brake block position.

   Brake levers should be positioned on the handlebars so
that they are capable of instantaneous operation with
comfort. On flat or raised handlebars such a position is
standard as there is only one position for the hands on
the bars; on dropped handlebars the most suitable
position is obtained when the brake lever assembly
clamps are fixed at the foremost point of the front bend
of the bars.

Wheels
Rims measuring 27″ in diameter and $1\frac{1}{4}$″ in width are
now almost universally used. They give a good

combination of responsiveness and reliability, and may be
of steel or alloy; steel is less likely to go appreciably out
of truth but is the more difficult to rectify should it do so.
However, this rarely happens. A deciding factor for many
tourists is again the weight saved by the use of alloy,
coupled with the appreciably more lively ride given by it.
Butted spokes are thin gauge for most of their length,
reinforced by ends of thicker gauge; for touring with a
weight aboard, standard spokes of thicker gauge
throughout are best.

The strength of any wheel lies in the accuracy with
which it has been built and trued, and occasional
attention by an experienced wheel builder will pay
dividends.

Hubs are also made in steel or alloy, and as both have a
very long life there is little to choose between them.
Lubrication is normally via a very inaccessible hole in the
middle of the body of the hub; it is needed every 500
miles or so, and when oiling you should lean the cycle
first one way and then the other so that the oil reaches
the bearings at both ends of the hub. 'Quick release' hubs
are expensive but virtually indestructible, require little
or no lubrication, and save a lot of trouble when it is
occasionally necessary to remove a wheel. They have
one-flip lever releases instead of the usual nuts at the
spindle ends.

Tyres, tubes and mudguards
Choose light tyres with a good patterned tread. Few cycle
tyres are now made in this country, but a good selection
of imported tyres is available. Inner tubes are mostly of
butyl, with valves like small-scale motor car tube valves.
Make sure that the pump connector supplied fits the
valves.

Tubular tyres are lightweight tubeless tyres fixed to

purpose-made rims with special cement and are designed
for cycle racing. They are ideal for this purpose but are
flimsy for touring purposes. The repair of punctures in
tubular tyres is a task needing skill and experience and is
not a job to be undertaken at the roadside. Light, plastic
mudguards are neat and adequate. A mudflap on the
front one will prevent you from splashing yourself when
it is wet, and a similar flap on the rear mudguard will be
appreciated by anyone riding behind you in such
conditions.

Chain
When correctly adjusted, there should not be more than
1″ free movement at the centre of the chain between the
chainwheel and sprocket. A little slack can be taken up
by loosening the rear wheel and pulling it back; a lot of
slack will involve the removal of a link (a special tool
which simplifies this task is a useful item of equipment).

Note that with derailleur gears a fully rivetted chain
must be used, and not one with a spring link connection.

Gears
Cycling has been aptly described as 'geared walking',
because the effort involved in walking a certain distance
will take one several times as far if used to propel a
bicycle.

The 'gear' of a bicycle is conventionally expressed in
inches, the number of inches being the diameter of an
imaginary wheel which would be turned one complete
revolution by one complete revolution of the pedals (that
is to say if it were a direct drive). This is a hand-down
from the days of the Ordinary (or 'penny farthing')
machine in which the pedals were attached directly to the
hub of the front wheel, which had a diameter of between
50″ and 60″, thus being the simplest form of direct drive,

and this sort of diameter being found about right for
pedalling rate, balance and modest gradients.

It is still about the right 'gear' for general use, but with
the advent of chain drive giving the possibility of
chainwheels and cogs having differing numbers of teeth,
a wide range of gears with smaller wheels naturally
followed.

So if you have a cycle with a chainring having twice as
many teeth as the rear sprocket, one turn of the pedals
will produce two turns of the wheels, and if the wheels
are 27″ in diameter, the imaginary wheel which would be
given a single turn would be 54″ in diameter – and that is
your gear. It's better than having a 54″ diameter wheel!

With the numerous sizes of chainrings and sprockets
that are now commonly available, a wide variety of

Gear mechanisms

derailleur type gear mechanisms offering between 3 and 6 different rear sprocket sizes, and the existence of double chainrings, an almost infinite selection of gearing is possible.

For touring, a range of gears is necessary to cope easily with all kinds of country – certainly three, preferably four or five, and, when you reach the pass-climbing stage, eight or ten, these involving a double chainring in addition to the rear 'block' having four or five cogs. Ideally, the gears will range between about 30″ and 90″. The aim is to maintain approximately the same pedalling rate whatever the speed of travel; the same rate at 5 m.p.h. uphill as at 25 m.p.h. on the level with a following wind! It is cycling which has given the language the wonderful word 'freewheeling', a downhill delight denied to those few riders who retain a preference for a single 'fixed' gear which means pedalling all the time.

With a chainwheel having 34 teeth, and rear sprockets (cogs) having 30, 23, 17, 13 and 11 teeth, gears of about 31″, 40″, 54″, 71″ and 83″ are obtained – a good range. The formula is simple: multiply wheel diameter (here 27″) by the number of chainwheel teeth and divide the result by the number of teeth on the rear sprocket.

A double chainwheel, with rings having 26 and 48 teeth, and rear sprockets having 28, 20, 18, 15 and 13 teeth give gears between 25″ and 100″ in good stages, and with this sort of combination no climb is formidable. The choice is wide, but the object of gearing must be kept in mind – to maintain your personal optimum pedalling rate at a constant comfortable level. Speed to the cycle tourist is not the primary consideration at all.

Triple chainrings are available. They require the use of an extended bottom bracket axle. Although three chainrings provide more choice of gears between top and bottom, some duplication of gears is inevitable and the selection of gears when riding is sometimes complicated. For these reasons, few tourists consider three chainrings to have any worthwhile advantage over two.

All gears of the kind described are operated by the popular 'derailleur' mechanism, the chain being moved from sprocket to sprocket by a guide pulley assembly operated by a lever normally situated handily on the down tube of the cycle frame. There are many varieties of derailleur gear of basically similar design and they all operate on widely differing sizes of sprocket. With double chainwheels a separate lever-operated mechanism moves the chain between the two wheels.

The limits of travel of the rear pulley assembly and the front chain cage are set by means of two adjusting screws on the mechanisms. When properly set, it is impossible for the chain to move beyond the limits of the chainrings or sprockets and become unshipped.

Hub gears, Sturmey Archer and the Japanese Shimano, have all the gear mechanism enclosed. It is an epicyclic arrangement and uses a single sprocket. They are highly reliable but in the rare event of a breakdown access to the complicated mechanism is difficult and diagnosis and repair equally so. They are available in 3-speed form only, the middle gear being of the order of 71", 63", 57" or 51". The top gear is 33% above the middle one, and the bottom gear 25% below it.

Lighting
Our lighting laws require the fitting of a reflector (red) and lamp (red) at the rear of the cycle and a lamp (white) at the front. They have to be of statutory design and performance. Equipped with these you will meet the requirements of other countries, but note that in most cases the lamps have to be fixed even if you intend to do

no night riding.

Manufacturers seem strangely unwilling to produce really robust and durable lamps, and those available of the battery-operated kind can only be described as of middling quality. Dynamo outfits are generally of better construction. A few have stand-by battery lamps which take over when the cycle is stationary. Battery lamps are sufficient for the average rider who does little night riding, and can be readily taken from the cycle for other uses (for example, in camp). Brackets for attaching the front lamp to the cycle are reasonably satisfactory. The design of fixing arrangements for rear lamps lacks imagination and some ingenuity is usually called for when mounting them, especially when pannier bags are used, so that the lamp does not obstruct the bags, and the bags do not obscure the beam.

How to ride

When riding, your weight should be roughly equally distributed between handlebars, saddle and pedals. Arms, posterior or legs will soon let you know if this is not the case so that any adjustment may be made which will eliminate their complaints, which should never be ignored.

From the start, cultivate a steady rhythm in riding – that is to say, a smooth pedalling action, the body moving neither from side to side nor forward and back as you ride. Observe other cyclists as you go about and you will note that they are sharply divided into those who have acquired this steady, easy action and those who have not. The latter are needlessly making heavy going of it and have yet to enjoy the art of cycling to the full. They will tire more quickly, and will not describe the straight line as they move along which is the natural result of correct riding position and technique. There is nothing mysterious about the acquisition of these but bad habits are not easy to correct and it is best to start off in the right way.

Never use too high a gear. For any condition of weather, road surface and gradient; select the gear which enables you to pedal without the exertion predominating over the pleasant sensation of wheeling along.

Never raise yourself out of the saddle to force the pedals round. It is bad style, reduces control of the cycle, and is uneconomical of effort. And it is unnecessary. Gear down. Or have a rest. Or have a walk. Why not?

Tandems

The popularity of tandem riding waxes and wanes; paradoxically, although few manufacturers are producing tandems at present, interest in them is increasing and the recently-formed Tandem Club reports a steadily rising membership.

There are few basic differences between a tandem and a solo machine. Frame tubing and tyres are heavier, because of the greater weight to be carried, and a tandem should have three brakes – a rear hub brake supplementing the usual two brakes acting on the rims. The extra braking power is needed because tandems gather great speed downhill; they are much faster than solos both downhill and on the level, but their weight and long wheelbase make them sluggish and slower on climbs.

Steering a tandem is an acquired art, and when cornering the steersman must remember the length of machine behind him. It is most important that the 'stoker' (the optimistic standard appellation for the rear rider) should simply grip the handlebars and make no attempt to steer or manoeuvre; to do so would be disastrous.

The rear chain is adjusted in the same way as on a solo cycle, but the adjustment of the front chain is by means of an eccentric bracket in the shell. Lockscrew and cotters are loosened, the bracket moved until the right tension is obtained, and the assembly tightened up again.

Most tandems are of 'double-gent' design though 'lady-backs' are also obtainable. Tandem pairs soon establish a common pedalling rhythm, and once this is obtained the 'team' makes smooth and efficient progress.

Tandems are a very good way of bringing the pleasures of cycling to those who would otherwise not be able to enjoy them. Elderly people can be taken for a spin on the back seat, and blind folk given much happiness in the same way, as well as those suffering other afflictions.

The luggage-carrying capacity of a tandem does not quite equal that of two solo machines, so that for touring a tandem couple will need front and rear panniers and a saddlebag, probably supplemented with a handlebar bag, to carry all their requirements.

Tricycles

The three-wheeler devotee can claim that this last difficulty is not one which he experiences, for between the rear wheels of a tricycle a very large bag can be carried, and front pannier bags and a handlebar bag can be fitted also if required.

Other advantages of the tricycle are its stability in bad weather conditions and the fact that the rider can stop without putting a foot to the ground. Against these, the width of the machine is a limitation on its manoeuvrability and denies it access to some narrow ways on which a bicycle can be taken. A tricycle is heavier than a solo machine, and has more 'drag' on the road.

A bicyclist taking up tricycling must learn to ride all over again. The technique is quite different; the rider of a tricycle must lean away from the curve and not into it as on a bicycle, and mastering this is not easy. Practice in a traffic-free road is essential until it is achieved, after which two wheels or three can be ridden with equal facility.

The majority of modern tricycles have single wheel drive to the nearside rear wheel, and derailleur gears in which the slack of the chain is taken up by the gear mechanism in the same way as on a bicycle. Single-speed tricycles, and tricycles fitted with hub gears, are rare, as are those with differential drives, where the two rear wheels are driven separately and at different speeds by means of an arrangement which was the forerunner of the differential drive on motor cars.

The rear axle is split centrally for the differential arrangement, and has a system of bevel wheels to balance the speed of the rear wheels. Adjustment of chain tension can be by means of telescopic chain stays or, more commonly, by the movement of a special eccentric bottom bracket assembly locked in the position which gives the right chain tension.

Conversion sets are available for transforming a bicycle into a tricycle. These permit of drive to one wheel only, and although a cheap and convenient way of finding out about tricycling they are not recommended; they are heavy and tend to 'whip' when ridden.

A tricycle has two brakes acting on the front wheel, as it is difficult to fit rim-acting brakes to the rear wheels. A hub brake and a rim brake are preferable to two rim brakes, although certain makes of the latter (notably *Mafac*, a French design) work very well one behind the other on the rim.

There are even tandem tricycles for those who like the best of both these worlds, providing that they can find someone else to share the fun!

Family cycling
Many parents take their children cycling, some of them

starting to do so when the children are very young. The most popular way of carrying a toddler on a cycle is in a 'kiddie-seat', a sort of miniature armchair carried over the rear wheel of the cycle behind the saddle, with supports securely fixed to the cycle frame. A child can be safely and prudently carried in this way from the age of about nine months.

The kiddie-seat precludes the use of rear cycle bags, so that all kit has to be carried in front bags (front panniers or handlebar bag or both). The bags at the front stabilise the cycle by counterbalancing the weight of the child at the back. A very small child is easily and securely carried in a small seat fixed to the crossbar of an adult's cycle (see illustration p. 34).

Less common are purpose-built sidecars and trailers for very young children. Such 'baby carriages' have not been manufactured commercially for some years, but as in the nature of things their period of individual usefulness is short, there is a brisk second-hand market in them. A competent handyman would not find it too formidable a task to build one himself.

The age at which a child becomes too heavy or too tall to be taken in a kiddie-seat is usually about five years, but can be up to seven years. When this stage is reached, parents turn to a tandem machine, either with a small 'junior-back' frame allowing the child to pedal normally, or with a special attachment at the back consisting of an extra (vertical) chain and chainring fitted with pedals at a height which the child can reach (see illustration p. 34).

Almost all of the bicycles marketed for the four to eight years age group are little more than toys – 'pavement cycles', usually (but not always) of heavy construction and with heavy tyres and accessories. Their main disadvantage is the very low gearing with which they are invariably supplied; it is this feature which makes them unsuitable for any but the most local rides as

Family cycling

the pedalling rate required is rapid and quickly fatiguing. They do, however, provide the means of learning how to balance on an individual cycle, and the first principles of cycle control.

By the age of eight or nine years most boys and girls are not only ready for their first 'real' bicycle but are eager to possess it. Few small-framed, lightweight, geared machines are readily available for them, but there are models which are suitable if some of the accessories and the gearing are changed. It is important that a child should ride a cycle of correct size and with appropriate equipment at all stages so that the ease and fun of good cycling are apparent and appreciated always.

Family cycling has its own techniques and its own rewards. Children, especially young ones, have their particular needs for food and clothing and impose a different routine from that of the adult tourist. Distances are reduced considerably both when carrying a small

All youngsters want a bicycle . . .

child in a kiddie-seat and when accompanying a larger
one on a separate machine. Children like to have a
frequent break for a romp or a run round. Parents who
take the family cycling enjoy themselves, and enjoy
seeing their children enjoying themselves. There are
'family sections' of the Cyclists' Touring Club in many
parts of the country, formed by families of cyclists to
exchange advice and help and to arrange rides and tours
to meet their own particular circumstances and wishes.

A note for the ladies

You do not have to be an Amazon to be a cycle tourist.
No out-of-the-ordinary physical strength is required, and
cycle-touring is enjoyed by women between the ages of
17 and 70 and by some even outside those limits.

They have found that with just a little regular riding
experience on the right machine with the right gears they
can go anywhere, and can go on going anywhere, settling
for distances to suit themselves, lingering at will and
relaxing in the freedom from a timetable existence.

Once you have experienced this freedom and
discovered the spirit of cycling and cyclists, you too will
want to go on cycling.

2

Before the tour

Riding experience

Few people can take up a new sort of physical activity, or
resume one after a lapse into inactivity, and find
themselves immediately proficient at it, or entirely
unaffected by it. Some preparation, or 'training', is
required. This is true of cycling, but the preparation is
very simple. All that is necessary is to ride – short
distances at first, increasing not to a set schedule but
simply in accordance with your own inclination – say,
beginning with five miles and working up to fifty. It
doesn't matter how long it takes, though it will probably
take a lot less time than you would imagine.

Unlike other pastimes, cycling needs no special
facilities. No special track or stadium, no expenditure for
instruction, no fixed timetable for outings. A few local
rides each week will quickly ensure harmony between
rider and cycle, slickness at changing gear, the discovery
of the right rate of pedalling, and not least a very
pleasant feeling of wellbeing.

If you are already a cyclist, all this will be well known
to you. If you are not, ask someone who is for instant
corroboration. Increasingly, commuters over daily
distances of up to ten miles each way are discovering the
less tangible advantages of cycling as well as the obvious
ones, and anyone who rides this sort of distance several
times a week will need little further training for touring.

Simple though the practical preparation is, it must not
be neglected. It is not unknown for would-be tourists to

purchase machines, to load them with equipment and set out for a fifty-mile ride for the first day of a tour.

They end up tired and disenchanted, and may possibly be heard spreading the rumour that cycling is 'hard work'.

No less important than the physical aspect of cycling is the psychology of it. The journey is every bit as important as the arrival, there being no question of reaching the destination as quickly as possible, or before the next man, or by the most direct route. It is this freedom from care and stress that marks cycling out as a uniquely restful way of touring and as the ideal antidote to the rat-race.

The question most frequently put to a cyclist who has covered any distance is 'How long did it take you?'; the answer is certainly that it doesn't matter, and probably that the longer it took the better!

Riding 'against the clock' is a deservedly popular form of cycle sport. It has no place in cycle touring. Never plan to do a greater distance than you know you can manage comfortably, and do not ride without a break until you begin to feel that you are no longer fully enjoying it. You will soon discover the best routine for your own ability and fancy, and that the more you ride the better you ride and the more you like riding.

It's all very personal, and there is perhaps no such animal as the 'average tourist'. But many will cover about 60 miles a day on tour in 'average' country (which will certainly include some hills) which represents some 5 or 6 hours' actual riding time, leaving adequate time for sightseeing, eating, or just being lazy. Some will get just as much pleasure from 25 miles a day, others will occasionally knock up the century. The one thing they will all have in common is that they will be enjoying themselves.

Checking the cycle

Having prepared yourself for touring, you must prepare
the bicycle. This equally straightforward process should
be carried out periodically in any case, and always before
embarking on a tour. There is little to go wrong with
such a simple machine which is inherently sturdy and has
components of great durability; with routine attention it
will give many years' faithful service.

Tyres should be checked for wear and pressure. The
tread of the rear tyre wears appreciably faster than that
of the front, as it carries most of the weight. It is a good
idea to change the tyres over when the rear one begins to
show signs of wear; at this time the front one will be very
little worn and will be almost as good as new on the rear
wheel; the one transferred from the rear to the front will
get very little further wear there. This changeover can
often be made with advantage during the course of a tour.

Cycle tyre pressures are surprisingly high – 70–80
lb./sq. in. – but pressure gauges are never used. Inflate
the tyres until they are almost 'brick hard' and they will
need little or no topping-up with air for a week.

Check wheels for truth; they should be perfectly round
and without a suspicion of buckle. Lifting from the
ground and spinning each wheel in turn, watching the
rim pass the brake block, is a simple way of seeing
whether the wheels are true. Wheel adjustment is a
skilled job and any necessary rectification should be
entrusted to an experienced mechanic. Once true, wheels
should remain so in normal use, but any slight maladjust-
ment will be accentuated with use.

Brake blocks should be checked for wear, and
replaced if necessary. Brake blocks slide into the shoes,
which are each secured by a single nut. Ensure that the
closed end of each brake shoe faces the direction of
travel when fixed.

Stranded wire cables operate the gears and brakes, and

the cables are enclosed for all or part of their lengths in an outer sleeving. They have a long life, but eventually they will fray, nearly always at a point where they suffer some abrasion in use – such as the point where the cable passes through a guide on the frame, or where it enters the brake or gear lever – and they should be replaced at the first sign of such fraying. Careful inspection is needed as the cables do not finally snap until the last couple of strands give way and it is easy to carry on blissfully ignorant of the fact that they are likely to go.

Lightly cover new cables with grease along all of their length before fitting. Brake cables should be fitted so that with the brake levers released the brake blocks are held $\frac{1}{16}''$ away from the rims. Gear cables should be taut but not tight when the lever is in the fully-forward position.

There should be no 'play' in the wheels at the hubs, i.e. no side-to-side movement of the wheel; at the same time it should not be too tight in the hub. This adjustment is made by means of a cone screwing on to the hub spindle beneath the locknut, the cone being loosened or tightened as required by means of a 'cone spanner'. The test is that, without any 'play', the wheel should rotate freely so that with the wheel off the ground the slight weight of the valve on the tube (protruding from the rim) should be sufficient to turn the wheel until the valve is at the bottom position.

Keep the cycle clean. A dirty machine is an inefficient one. The mere process of going over all the parts of it with a cloth draws attention to any odd loose nut, etc. and any such discoveries can be given immediate attention.

Lubricate here and there as required; note that the chain can very easily be given too much oil. It needs only just enough to keep it running smoothly. More will merely collect dust and dirt and cover the chain with a thick, dirty deposit and have the reverse effect to that intended.

3

Taking the bicycle for a ride

A wide variety of interesting excursions can be made at weekends, but most holiday cycle tours are of one to three weeks' duration and most cycle tourists will want to visit a distant area either in this country or abroad. To reach the selected area the cycle must be taken for a ride.

Many cyclists are also car-owners and for them the problem can be solved by carrying the machines on a roof-rack. Some standard racks will accommodate cycles satisfactorily, and there are racks of special design which will transport up to four machines. The chief disadvantage of this method of reaching the touring area is that the tour will normally have to end at the point at which it began, that is to say, where the car has been left. The alternative is the use of public transport for cycles and riders, which presents no difficulties and avoids the necessity of the tour being a round trip.

In this country, 'public transport' means rail or air – in some countries abroad, as noted in the appropriate section of this book, it also includes bus. With very few exceptions (which need not concern us) cycles are carried by all British Railways trains at a charge which is half of the second class adult fare with an upper maximum charge for the cycle. This rate is for accompanied cycles, and applies equally to reduced rate passenger tickets such as day, weekend and period returns.

The ticket is purchased at the station or travel agent in the same way as the passenger ticket, and the passenger is expected to put the machine in the guard's van himself and to unload it at the destination station. It should be labelled with the name of the destination station and with the owner's name and address.

The lack of attention on the part of British Railways has the advantage that one can usually park the cycle to one's satisfaction in the van (it is a good idea to lash it with a cord or elastic expander to a convenient point in the van so that there is no possibility of its falling over en route), and can reclaim it without delay on arrival.

In continental countries the charge for carrying cycles by train is very much lower, varying according to distance up to about £1.50 for a single journey. The cycle, minus bags and detachable items such as lamps and pump, must be handed in as registered baggage at the departure station an hour before the train goes, and the fee paid. It is collected from the baggage arrival depot at the destination station, usually being available there within twenty minutes of the train's arrival. The receipt given for the cycle at the start of the journey has to be surrendered in exchange for it at this point.

Normally the cycle will travel on the continent by the same train as the passenger accompanying it although in the high season the railway authorities do not guarantee this. To avoid the most irksome possibility of reaching your destination and finding the cycle is travelling twenty-four hours or so behind you, make sure at busy times that the official receiving the cycle at the departure station knows which train you are catching; in case of language difficulty write it down, or better still show him your seat reservation ticket (which gives this information), and he will usually be found co-operative.

If you can get to the station to register the cycle(s) more than the required one hour in advance of the train departure time, do so; at busy times there may be a delay in registration and in any case it helps the railway staff if they have a little longer to handle the cycles. If the continental journey involves crossing a frontier, the cycles have to be cleared by the Customs after – sometimes at the same time as – registration. This involves the minimum of formality and no special documentation.

Cycles may be registered from London railway termini to any major station on the continent which has customs clearance facilities. After registration in London the machines are taken to the Customs shed from where they are loaded direct into a luggage van which is sealed until opened by customs officials abroad.

If, however, your journey from London to the continent with your cycle involves travel via Paris, Brussels or Basel and a change of train or travel between termini at one of those places for the onward connection, register the cycle only to that place, registering it again for the second leg of the journey. This is most important, for otherwise it is highly unlikely that your cycle will make the same change of train as you do and it will not arrive at your ultimate destination until at least a day later.

Equally, on a return journey to London involving a change of train at one of the cities mentioned, register the cycle that far only and make a second registration thence to London, or again you will arrive at least a day before your cycle – very awkward if you had planned to ride away from the arrival station.

Cycles may also be registered from the port of embarkation in England to continental destinations in the same way, if, for example, you ride to the port or take the cycle there by car to pick the vehicle up again on your return.

Taking a cycle from a channel port to ports in France or Belgium is very simple, a matter of buying the tickets for yourself and the machine and going through the simple customs procedures. On sailings to Holland and

Scandinavia, and on some British or French Railways operated sailings in high summer to France and Belgium, booking in advance is strongly recommended as the boats will be full and their capacity is limited by statute.

Cycles are conveyed too by the more frequent, often cheaper car ferries run by several operators from Southampton and a number of Kent ports and they and their riders are accepted cheerfully and at short notice.

Cycles are readily taken by air. For travel entirely within the British Isles, there is a nominal charge of 50p by British Airways and most other airlines for journeys up to 200 miles, and of £1 for longer distances. Internal airlines which do not conform with this tariff charge the usual excess baggage rate if the total weight of cycle and luggage exceeds the 33 lb. free allowance.

In all cases cycles should be taken to the airport – not the city air terminal – at least one hour before departure time. On some flights, restricted baggage space may result in a cycle being unacceptable unless prior agreement has been reached, but this does not often happen. It may, however, be requested by the airport staff that the front wheel be removed (and tied to the frame) and the handlebars and pedals turned, so as to make the machine more compact for stowage.

Accompanied cycles are carried free on international flights within the 44 lb. allowance, excess being payable only if the combined weight of cycle and luggage exceeds this.

Air ferries carrying vehicles and passengers operate from Southend to coastal airports in France, Belgium and Holland and to Basel in Switzerland, on which no dismantling of cycles or unloading of baggage is ever required. Reservations for these services must be made well in advance.

Insurance

Cycles should always be insured against damage or theft. Never leave a cycle unattended and unlocked, and do not leave the key to the lock or any valuables in one of the cycle bags. The cost of insurance is not high but the peace of mind is great.

Members of the Cyclists' Touring Club are insured free against possible third-party claims, covering them when cycling anywhere in the world in respect of claims up to £250,000. The C.T.C. also offers all other insurances at favourable rates. Claims are dealt with speedily and sympathetically by its own Insurers.

Short-term holiday insurances, covering medical and other expenses, personal legal liability and cancellation or curtailment charges in addition to the risks already mentioned, are available at a modest cost for 17 days, increasing pro rata for longer periods.

4

What to take

The amount of kit which can be carried by bicycle is
limited, and the weight and bulk of it must be kept to a
minimum. No superfluous items should be packed. This
does not mean that an adequate wardrobe, personal
belongings and a supply of spares cannot be carried for
any length of tour – one cyclist who rode to Australia
used a Moulton cycle the all-up weight of which was
45 lb., and he needed rather more equipment and supplies
than are required by the weekend or fortnight tourist.

Clothing

Two basic outfits are needed – one for wear when
cycling and the other to change into when you stop. A
reserve set of each, making four outfits in all, ensures
that there will be no problems should clothing become
wet in the rain or inadvertently soiled with grease or
mud.

All clothing should be lightweight and capable of
being folded up small. (Folding is more economical on
space than rolling.) Lavish use of plastic bags containing
individual items or groups of like items (e.g. socks)
facilitates location in the cycle bags and keeps the
contents clean.

Articles made of nylon and other man-made fibres have
the advantages of lightness and small bulk, and will dry
overnight, but they do not equal natural cotton and wool
for warmth and versatility.

Shorts are the ideal wear for cycling in weather, from
cool to hot, with a light shirt. This should be supplemented

with a woollen pullover or sweater as required. White socks look and feel good when cycling.

A pair of 'longs' of some sort is essential. You may wish to wear them in the evening, even if it is warm, although informal wear, including shorts, is now almost universally acceptable in Europe for holidaymakers.

Light, narrow shoes should be worn which are not wider than the pedals. They can double for evening wear, but it is preferable from the points of view of both hygiene and comfort to have a complete change of outfit, and an additional pair of sandals or plimsolls is recommended.

It will be seen that most people will already have enough of the sort of clothing suitable for cycling without having to make purchases of special wear. Tennis shorts, or shorts used for rambling or scouting, are perfectly satisfactory for cycling. So are leisure shirts, and sports socks, and the usual run of woollen wear. The outer garment can be the kind of poplin or nylon jacket as used for golf, boating or general spare-time wear.

There is, however, a wide range of clothing specially made for the rider who has decided that cycling is such fun that he wants to equip himself specifically for it in the same way that he would for any other pastime.

Starting at the bottom, cycling shoes are specially low-cut leather affairs with a thin sole and low heel. Their pliable uppers have strategically placed patches, the whole idea being to cope with the particular stresses imparted by the motion of pedalling. They are extremely comfortable, and it is possible to have metal or plastic plates fixed to the soles with slots which locate on the pedals. Shoe-plates eliminate slipping on the pedal but have certain drawbacks for the tourist which

To Australia by Moulton bicycle

probably outweigh the slight advantage. They make walking somewhat awkward, and they are unkind to carpets and flooring, which can be an embarrassment when visiting or even when shopping. In particular the rider who uses toe-clips will find that the slight extra pedal grip afforded by shoe-plates is not really worth the extra trouble.

Shorts especially for cycletouring are made in whipcord, khaki, denim and even leather, which is very comfortable for riding – natural materials again. They are usually a little longer in the body than shorts for other activities so that the lower part of the back is covered when leaning forward in the riding position.

If it is preferred to keep the legs covered, special 'longs' for cycling are much better than ordinary trousers, which are never fashioned in a way which avoids either bagginess or tightness when riding. The bottoms can easily get badly soiled from contact with the chain or chainring or both; a tourist using trouser clips is a very rare sight because they are ineffective for a ride of any distance.

Favourite garments for cycletouring therefore are 'plusses' – trousers ending with elastic or a buckle just below the knee and worn with long socks – a very neat combination. Plusses are made with varying amounts of fullness in the upper leg to suit varied preferences.

There is nothing special about shirts for cycletouring, though for men the tunic pattern has an advantage in that the amount of ventilation is infinitely adjustable with it.

Racing cyclists have a whole range of clothing specially designed and tailored for their sport and much of it is excellent for touring wear as well. Racing shorts are of wool or nylon or a mixture of both and have a chamois leather patch in the crucial place inside. They are black, have an elastic waistband and are close fitting, and are very comfortable in use.

Track suits also come in the same materials and in a variety of colours. The bottom halves are ideal for those who like to cover their legs at all times, and for all riders in cooler conditions of weather. They, and the upper jackets, are also close fitting and will withstand unlimited folding and packing without losing their shape.

Racing 'vests' are really shirts with long or short sleeves, made of cotton or nylon, in various thicknesses and either plain or multi-coloured. Some have pockets along the bottom at the back of the garment, intended for the essential needs of the racing cyclist when taking part in an event, but equally useful for the tourist wanting to keep map, handkerchief, etc. handy all the time.

'What do you do if it rains?' is a frequent question, and wherever you go touring you must be prepared for some rain. It is more likely to occur in northern Europe than in the sunny lands of the south, but it would be a supreme optimist who decided to dispense with rainwear altogether for a tour – remember you will be returning to Britain where you may well need it, anyway!

The ideal rainwear for cycling has yet to be invented, but it is possible to keep dry when riding in the wet except perhaps in the greatest deluge. At least one can keep drier than when walking. The standard equipment is the familiar cape – the yellow British cape is unique and readily recognised abroad – and waterproof headgear, which can be the trusty sou'wester (the only thing which will assuredly prevent water from running down the back of your neck) or a cap (a nylon yachting-type peaked cap is very effective). Capes have a tape fixed inside the back, to tie round the waist, and thumb loops inside at the front – both features are designed to prevent the cape blowing up over the head. Neither idea is very effective; the thumb loops are not popular as they restrict control of the cycle. It is therefore a good idea to sit on the tail of the cape when it is in use.

The alternative to the cape is a nylon anorak with a hood. Its advantages are that one article covers both head and body, and it has sleeves, which afford better manoeuvrability. The disadvantage is that the anorak is not long enough to stop some water running on to one's shorts or legs. Any cyclist will tell you, by the way, that wet legs are better than wet trousers when riding; they certainly dry more quickly, and many cycle tourists do not trouble very much about the occasional wetting of the lower limbs when they get a shower on tour.

But full-length, very lightweight, overtrousers are available, as are short 'spattee' waterproofs which cover the shoes and the legs to the knee. They are kept in position by several elastic loops with press studs. They are the only items offering protection to the feet – though in fact the feet do not get as wet as would be expected when cycling in the rain save in unusually prolonged or heavy showers.

A plastic overshoe ending just above the ankle is not practical and not effective; it quickly chafes and tears on the pedal, and the water just enters at the top.

An unwillingness to be out in the rain would seem to be a fairly recent phenomenon. Cycling in the rain is not at all unpleasant if one is correctly prepared for it both in clothing and attitude, and on occasion can be a positive relief!

The shorts or 'plus-twos' – a neater version of plus-fours – the shirt or blouse, the ankle socks and cycling shoes – all are common to both sexes and are very practical wear for touring. Some ladies may prefer a skirt to shorts, and this is ideal providing the skirt is pleated to allow for leg movement. An anorak or windcheater with a zipped front is essential as an outer garment. Most are showerproof and windproof, and they can be stowed into the saddlebag when not in use or strapped to the outside of the bag.

For really wet weather cape and sou'wester are best, but some ladies prefer something a little more feminine than the latter; there are plenty of rain hats on the market – but one must remember to choose one of the sort which ties on. In at least one respect the ladies have the edge on the men when it comes to cycling. They like, perhaps, to give more attention to their apparel when off the bike – in the evenings, or when sightseeing. Carrying an adequate wardrobe for such occasions seems to present no problem with the availability of a wide range of lightweight, non-crush garments. The usual cycle bags are capable of carrying a sufficient selection for even the fastidious.

The cycle tourist is in a different place and among different people if not every evening, then very nearly so; there is no possibility of the same people seeing you in the same outfit day after day! So you have to cater only for your own liking for changes of wear; it is amazing what a considerable variety of clothing a lady is able to carry, without unreasonably increasing the weight to be carried or experiencing any difficulty in packing it all away.

Spares and tools
The bicycle is such a simple and reliable machine that a breakdown of a more serious kind is most unlikely to occur on a tour. Even a 'more serious' breakdown when applied to a cycle is unlikely to involve much difficulty or delay, given average mechanical ability and a basic understanding of the way a bicycle works.

Every tourist in Britain should carry:
Puncture repair outfit, complete with tyre levers. The
cause of the puncture, and hence the location of it, is
often obvious; if it is not, a slight inflation of the inner
tube will normally enable you to hear the air escaping
from the puncture and quickly to locate it.
Spanner(s), either the flat, adjustable type or the
'dumbell' pattern, to fit all nuts on the machine. Regular
checks for tightness should be made on all nuts with
these, and they may be needed for removal of parts.
Spoke key (or spanner) for minor adjustments to loose
spokes and the removal of broken spokes and fitting of
new ones.
Small leak-proof can of oil, spare front and rear brake
cables (inner wires only), spare gear cables, four spare
spokes, two spare brake blocks.

The tourist going abroad should take, in addition to the
above, a spare inner tube and outer tyre (British sizes are
not easy to obtain abroad), freewheel remover, chain
rivet extractor and a few spare links of chain.

It is always well to carry a few spare nuts and bolts of
various sizes and a length of strong but pliable wire.

The variety of cycle parts and equipment manufactured
in Britain has declined considerably in recent years, and
components and accessories made and used abroad are
increasingly used on British machines. One effect of this
trend which is to the advantage of the cycle tourist is
that the likelihood is increased of being able to obtain
suitable replacement parts if needed when abroad.

Cycle shops selling standard items are found in all
towns and cities of any size in this country and in most
continental ones (see under individual countries).
Dealers with workshops able to undertake repairs are less
common, and are in any case not always able to provide
immediate service. Many places, even quite small ones,

have a 'little man' who stocks a limited range of spares
and who may even be ready and willing to help with
repairs.

In general, help for the cyclist with mechanical
trouble is more readily forthcoming abroad than it is at
home. There, cycling is a good deal more respected, and
more interest is shown in the cyclist and his steed than is
customary here. Help should always be sought on the
continent from any likely source – garage, blacksmith,
cycle shop, etc.

All that being said, it must be added that it is usually
the case that all the spares and tools are carried but not
required, so reliable is the bicycle and so rare any
difficulties of any consequence. But experience also
shows that the surest way of needing one or other of the
bits and pieces is to travel without them, so on no
account neglect to check that they are safely stowed
before setting off.

5

How to take it

The bicycle not only very smoothly makes your own effort transport you, it also carries all you need. Never, but never, carry anything on your back; even a small bag on the back when riding is uncomfortable, generates heat and slides about. It can also disturb your control of the machine. Some tourists will break this rule in order to carry their camera at the ready, but even a camera around the person may become an irritation.

For carrying kit on a cycle there are saddlebags, rear pannier and front pannier bags, and handlebar bags. Only tourists who wish to carry a lot of special equipment – for example, a range of photographic accessories, or supplies of sketching and painting materials – will use all of these at once; for the average tourist it is a matter of choosing two or three bags to suit his own preferences.

A saddlebag is almost invariably the main carrier. Saddlebags come in various sizes, the largest of which will hold enough kit for a week's tour in summer without any other bags being needed. Alternatively, for shorter tours, a small saddlebag with front or rear panniers can be used, enabling the load to be 'departmentalised', an advantage if you are lucky enough to be able to remember first time what is in which bag.

Rear panniers are quite commodious, usually being about a foot square and six inches deep back to front. Like saddlebags, they have small end pockets which are convenient for packing a few small things to which access should be easy at all times – puncture repair outfit, spanner and screwdriver, first-aid kit, etc. Some panniers are tapered downwards, making them neater and better fitting but at the expense of a little space.

Special frames are needed to carry the pannier bags over the rear wheel, and similarly over the front wheel if so desired. If you are ordering a bicycle specially for touring, you should ask for lugs to be brazed on the cycle frame during manufacture to which the pannier frame(s) can be bolted. These lugs will be near the top of each seat stay and at the top of each fork end for rear panniers, and above the front fork ends for front panniers.

Pannier carrier frames so bolted to the cycle frame

Carrier for front pannier bags.

make for a very rigid assembly, though they can be fitted quite satisfactorily to an ordinary cycle frame by means of metal clips bolted round the top of the seat stays (for rear bags) and extension pieces bolted between the wheel spindles (front and rear bags) and the bottom of the pannier carriers.

All pannier carriers should be of steel and basically triangular in shape. Alloy frames are not strong enough, sometimes cracking under weight and vibration, and square ones can lose their shape. The triangle is the strongest mechanical construction and carriers so shaped invite the use of tapered bags for a neat ensemble. For use with square bags, a triangular carrier should have additional framework to prevent the possibility of the bags fouling the spokes; another way of guarding against this is to fit thin wood or metal strips along the inside rear lower edge of the bags.

If rear pannier bags are correctly fitted, the heel should never touch them when pedalling. A small strap may be needed to hold them in position so that they do not edge forward when riding, the strap being placed tightly round the top straps of the panniers and the top crosspiece of the carrier.

Front pannier bags are the same as rear ones only smaller. They spread the load more evenly about the cycle but make the steering a bit heavy until one gets accustomed to them. They are handy for carrying every-day things like toilet kit, maps and chocolate.

Handlebar bags sit between the bends of the bars, strapped to the straight section of them by two or three short straps, with a lower strap for looping round the head tube. Care must be taken to ensure that a handlebar bag does not rest upon the brake cables – which might hold the brakes on and will certainly make them very unresponsive – and does not rest upon the front mudguard, which would certainly cause it to scrape the front tyre. Special brackets can be obtained to prevent these occurrences, but they all add weight and in general handlebar bags are not popular among British tourists – though it is fair to add that continental and American tourists view them more favourably.

A handlebar bag will often include a transparent pocket on the top for carrying the map in use. A small, neat map clip for this purpose is equally practical and is bolted under the head of the central handlebar fixing bolt (it will not fit handlebars which use an Allen-head type bolt at this point).

The traditional material for cycle bags is heavy black duck (heavy in the trade sense only – in fact the bags are remarkably light in weight) with chrome leather straps. They are unequalled for their waterproof and longlasting

Touring cycle complete with saddlebag, front and rear panniers and handlebar bag

properties and will give several years of intensive use. Proofed nylon bags are gaining in popularity, but although they are slightly lighter in weight their thin material makes them 'floppy'. Some cheap bags are made from plastic, or fabric with plastic beading; these are quite unsuitable for touring use as they split or tear at the slightest provocation.

For carrying food purchased for early consumption, and such things as phrase books, sunglasses and even cigarettes if you use them, a simple shoulder-type bag (or racing cyclists' *musette*, which is much the same thing) is conveniently slung around the saddle pin and allowed to rest on top of the saddlebag, kept in place by an elastic expander.

One soon gets accustomed to packing belongings in the bags in a regular routine way. General hints are to try to keep each bag for a specific group of articles – outer clothing in one, underwear, socks, handkerchiefs in another, sandals and tools in another. Few things are incompatible, especially if things like soap and after-shave are carried in plastic bags or containers, and if you can manage with just one bag or two, do so.

The camera will travel perfectly safely in the *musette*, and be readily to hand there; the *musette* can be rapidly removed and shouldered if you leave the cycle for a while – say when shopping. For longer periods when it is not in use, the camera can be carefully wrapped in a pullover or towel and carried well packed in the saddlebag.

6

Maps

The most important thing about a map is the scale to which it is drawn. Upon this depends how much information can be shown; clearly, very little information can be crowded onto a map on which one inch represents ten miles, whilst a very great deal can be given with a scale of one inch to one mile, by the use of conventional symbols and indications the meaning of which can be readily grasped.

Publishers in this country are at present engaged in the lengthy process of reissuing all their maps converted to metric scales from our traditional Imperial scale. The metric system is used everywhere else in Europe already, and this is part of our national policy of metrication. Some Imperial scale maps are still published pending the change, and many will continue in use for some years after the change has been completed, so it is as well to give a table of scales:

Scale	Metric	Imperial
1:25,000	1 cm = 250 m	$2\frac{1}{2}''$ = 1 mile
1:50,000	1 cm = 500 m	$1''$ = $\frac{3}{4}$ mile
1:100,000	1 cm = 1 km	$1''$ = $1\frac{1}{2}$ miles
1:200,000	1 cm = 2 km	$1''$ = $3\frac{1}{4}$ miles
	and so on	

For the general outline planning of a cycling tour, a map on a scale of 1:625,000 (1 cm = 6·25 km, or about ten miles to the inch) will be required. To give some idea of the coverage of maps on this scale, two sheets will cover the whole of Britain. But they must be *maps*, that is to say, they must at least show the contours of the land and give some indication of population density and the road network.

Very many maps are available which are no more than road diagrams, and diagrams of major roads at that. They fulfil very well their purpose of showing the fast traveller – the motorist or the goods vehicle driver – the quickest or most direct routes from place to place, but they give little or no information beyond that. They will give no mental picture of the terrain they cover, no indication of the network of minor roads and lanes and will name only the larger cities and towns to the exclusion of villages, landmarks and natural features.

Such maps are useless to the cycle tourist, but true maps to this scale are published by the Ordnance Survey and John Bartholomew and Son Ltd., which are widely available from bookshops and stationers. Similar maps are produced for almost all of the rest of Europe by various continental publishers. Styles vary but all are easily understood; all maps on scales of use to cyclists have a complete explanation of the signs and symbols used on every sheet.

Maps like these give a good overall impression of the selected touring area from the points of view of scenery, less-used roads, gradients and population, which are the chief things one wants to know when considering the best route to take, the daily distance to ride, and possible places to stop for refreshment and accommodation.

For route-finding when actually on the road, maps with still more detail are needed, and the most suitable for this purpose are those to a scale of between 1 : 100,000 and 1 : 200,000. Each map sheet on these scales will cover an area approximately 80 km × 80 km (50 miles each way) and 160 km × 160 km (100 miles each way) respectively; the map sheets themselves measure some 80 cm (32") square. These details vary a little between publishers and countries.

Bartholomews are now issuing their maps in metric and call their new series the 'National Map Series, scale 1:100,000'. The new sheets are appearing in numerical order (working through Britain from south to north) and all sheets should be replaced with a metric version by the end of 1976.

The British Ordnance Survey at present publishes 1:50,000 scale map sheets covering England and Wales south of a line joining Morecambe and Bridlington, replacing the 1" to 1 mile series which was current until 1974. For the north of England and Scotland, the 1" to 1 mile sheets are still current, but they will be replaced by the new metric sheets in 1976.

These maps are very detailed and are ideal for tracing a cycling way using minor roads, choosing the best scenic route, judging distances and hence time likely to be taken, and they will enable cycle tourists to capture the pleasure and satisfaction of quiet, joyous travel which are theirs alone. These maps will also reveal some popular fallacies – for example, that a lane following a valley must necessarily be flat; it isn't true!

Not that all cyclists choose the less hilly roads; hills and mountains 'make' the scenery and not a few cycle tourists choose the ridge roads and mountain passes as a matter of policy and gain great enjoyment and exhilaration by so doing.

Details of maps recommended for individual countries are given under the information about each one in chapter 10. Although maps published abroad vary a little in style and presentation from our own, the above remarks apply equally to them. They are all extremely well designed and informative and repay study;

'reading' a map becomes a significant term and doing so is most rewarding, whether one is excitedly anticipating a tour, engaged upon it, or looking back on its many and varied happenings.

The map on page 64 shows part of suggested tour No. 6 (page 232). The main road from the north to le Puy is the N 106 through Bellevue, but the unhurried cycle tourist chooses the minor roads through Craponne-sur-Arzon to Retournac and the gorges of the Loire – almost all of these roads having the green edging on the map indicating routes of scenic beauty. (Map taken from Michelin 1 : 200,000 series, sheet 76, 4th edition, and reproduced by permission of the publishers, Pneu Michelin, Paris.)

The cycle tourist has a typical variety of minor roads from which to choose a route between Totnes and Kingsbridge when touring in south Devon. He might ride to Ashprington, Blackawton and East Allington (towards Kingsbridge), a quiet, scenic meander with several lanes leading down to the coast if he feels like a swim. These easily-discovered ways avoid the main roads and take in quiet villages and lovely countryside. (Map on page 65 taken from National Map Series 1 : 100,000, sheet 2, South Devon, and reproduced by permission of John Bartholomew & Son Ltd., Edinburgh.)

7

On tour

Distance
The agreeable facts are that it doesn't matter how many miles you cover on a cycling tour, and it doesn't matter how fast you go. You are free to please yourself, to go where you want at your own pace and to stop as often as you like. Relaxation and freedom from care are the lot of the cycle tourist.

A few half-day or day rides from home will soon demonstrate the truth of these statements. Even if you live in a big city there will be much nearby territory with which you are probably unacquainted, and which can be explored at weekends when commuters and traffic are at their least – and few people live more than an hour's easy riding from the countryside.

If you don't want to 'go it alone' there are others like you with whom you could team up – or, better still, get in touch with the local section of the Cyclists' Touring Club, which will normally have regular local rides arranged for cyclists of all tastes and abilities and of both sexes. There may even be a 'family' section too. This way most of the preparatory work is done for you and you will meet people who already enjoy touring.

You should base your daily tour mileages on the knowledge gained in this way, never planning to cover more ground than you know you can do without fatigue. You can always ride a bit further than planned if you wish when the time comes.

You may sometimes get tired, and you will certainly sometimes get hungry, but these are quite natural and

proper conditions for healthy men and women! A
fortnight's typical holiday cycle tour can be of anything
between 400 and 1,000 miles in length. It depends
entirely on the inclination of the rider or riders
concerned. It cannot be too strongly emphasised that the
fun and interest of a cycling tour are in no way related to
the distance covered.

Many cyclists will deliberately plan a 'rest day' now
and again during the tour – days on which no riding is
planned with two consecutive nights spent at the same
place. Perhaps they will make a short local ride on the
intervening day if they feel like it, leaving most of their
kit behind for the day. Or they may decide to make a tour
of a town or city on foot; the possibilities are numerous
and once again the cyclist is in the pleasant position of
being able to please himself.

Food

Whether any change in eating habits will be found
desirable depends on those normally followed. If you
usually have a cooked breakfast, you will perhaps find
that you cannot do without it, although many tourists
have been surprised how far they can ride on a
continental breakfast of coffee and rolls, which on the
face of it is little enough on which to take to the road. It
is, however, never wise to ride immediately after a meal
of any size, so always allow a good half-hour between
anything more than a snack and setting off again.

For this reason, as well as to simplify the daily
organisation, it is a good idea – especially in warm
weather – to let a picnic or two during the day satisfy the
needs of the inner cyclist. Apart from the digestive
problems, it is certainly psychologically less easy to
resume distance riding in the replete condition
experienced after a three (or more) course lunch.

So the main meal of the day should be taken in the evening, after the day's riding is over. It will make a fitting conclusion to an eventful day, can be indulged in without any worries about digestion, and afterwards the next day's touring can be arranged with an agreeable sense of anticipation by looking over the maps and deciding the approximate route to be followed and things to be done subject to inclination when the time comes.

Taking the substantial meal of the day in the evening may well explain why it is often found that a small breakfast next day goes a long way.

'Tummy trouble' is sometimes suffered by tourists abroad, and for cyclists is particularly disrupting. It need never happen. The usual items of food abroad are just the same as they are here. It is the consumption of these usual items cooked or prepared in a way to which we are not accustomed, or of foods to which the system is not accustomed, which causes tummies to respond in an unaccustomed way. Yet, for a lot of us, one of the reasons for going abroad is to sample the local dishes – and the local beverages! The answer is to be sensible. Sample these foods and drinks in moderation. Especially if you are sensitive to changes of diet, stick to the unadorned food which you are used to most of the time.

There survives a widespread suspicion of the purity of water abroad. It is almost entirely unfounded. Village wells, pumps and springs produce good drinking water with very few exceptions, and the exceptions are marked with notices, e.g. 'Eau non potable' (not drinking water) in France. For greatest assurance, a supply of water purification tablets can be taken from the U.K. or the water boiled. Common sense and personal cleanliness are the chief weapons against stomach disorders, but should one occur due to food or drink a tablet of enterovioform or something similar taken twice a day will usually clear it up. In the unlikely event of persistent trouble, medical advice should be sought, but it is emphasised that such a condition is avoidable and is certainly not likely to afflict the cyclist any more than any other traveller.

Accommodation

The idea of taking oneself off on holiday without the least notion of where the overnight stopping places are going to be strikes many people as novel, or risky, or even foolhardy, but many cycle tourists do just that very successfully, proving that these reactions are not justified.

Booking in advance ties you down and to some extent limits the freedom of movement on which so much store is set. It means that every effort must be made to honour the bookings, even if you find a particularly pleasant place elsewhere that you would like to stop at, or if you are not able to cycle comfortably as far as anticipated, or if hobbies pursued on the way occupy more time than you thought they would.

Against these considerations, some cyclists prefer to know that their beds await them at the end of each day and will not have to be sought.

In the vast majority of places at home and abroad there is no need to fear being unable to find accommodation 'on spec'. However, the English Lake District, the north of Scotland, and the much frequented resorts from Blackpool to Nice and Dubrovnik, will for example be bursting at the seams in August, as will Salzburg at Festival time, and if you want to stay in these and similar places at peak periods then booking quite a long time ahead is essential.

Few cycle tourists will want to do so. If they wish to go to popular places and particular local events, they will visit them by day and retire for the night to a hamlet or small town five or ten miles distant, where rooms in

hotels and pensions are usually available. The proprietors
will give a special welcome, and will appreciate the
discrimination shown by those who prefer to stay in the
peace of their locality and to avoid the crowds. And it
will be less costly.

Elsewhere little difficulty in finding accommodation
each night will be experienced. For cyclists touring in
Britain, the C.T.C. publishes annually a handbook (for
members only) listing guest-house and hotel addresses
'appointed' by the Club where they will be welcome.
This handbook also contains a wealth of general
information about cycle touring and travel, maps,
insurances, etc. both at home and abroad.

The British Tourist Authority publishes regional guides
which contain accommodation lists, and many local
authorities also issue lists for their own districts. Tourist
enquiry centres are increasing in number in Britain,
especially in Scotland, where in the summer months they
are to be found in most places of any size or importance
ready to advise on accommodation possibilities in the
area.

On the continent they do things rather better for the
tourist. The national tourist offices in London of each
country will supply a general or regional guide and
accommodation list on request. Enquiry offices are
commonly found on the continent waiting to help;
municipal offices almost everywhere will also be helpful.
In France the local office to look for is called the *Syndicat
d'Initiative*, to be found in any place of any size at all.

These services are really a last resort and will rarely be
needed. There are far more small hotels and *pensions*
abroad than in Britain, and the occasional traveller is far
more common. There will usually be several places to
stay from which to make a choice – another advantage of
not booking ahead, when little or no idea of the type of

accommodation or its surroundings can be obtained.

The reception accorded to cyclists abroad is very kind and considerable interest is often shown in their plans and activities.

There is a vast network of youth hostels in Europe and a membership card of the Youth Hostels Association of one's country of residence admits the holder to all those in the International Federation, without further formality. Each country issues annually a handbook (in the language of the country) listing all the hostels and applicable rules. An International Handbook is also produced every spring. This comes in two parts, one for Europe and the Mediterranean and one for the rest of the world. They have essential information in English and employ internationally-used symbols for details of each hostel and its facilities.

A group of cycle tourists leaving Bellingham youth hostel, Northumberland

Hostels are graded according to the facilities provided at each: simple, standard and superior are the terms used. The amenities offered, and the cost, are higher as the standard rises. They receive intense usage, mainly by groups, and individuals and small parties should book accommodation in advance during July and August (at any time of the year at hostels in major cities and holiday resorts). At many of them, meals can be provided by the warden if booked in advance, and at most of them self-catering facilities are provided. Most countries still require those staying overnight at hostels to share modest domestic duties voluntarily, although in a few this rule is now honoured more in the breach than in the observance.

Whilst youth hostels in most countries are open to people of all ages, over five years old, there is a maximum age limit of 25 in Switzerland and 27 in Bavaria; in some countries preference is given to younger members in the event of available accommodation being limited. In Britain, the Scandinavian countries, and Belgium, some youth hostels have special rooms for families with young children.

There is a certain 'mystique' about youth hostelling and some experience of it at home is recommended before hostelling abroad. It provides communal and inexpensive living for tourists of all kinds.

Anyone thinking about a cycle tour for the first time may have a few apprehensions. What happens if my cycle breaks down? What happens if I come across a particularly difficult road? If I get lost? If there is a sudden storm? If I can't find a shop when I want one? There is no end to the things which you think might go wrong but the significant point is that you will not find an experienced cycle tourist worrying about them and it will not be long before you appreciate that such worries are unfounded.

It is rare for anything at all to go wrong. It is rarer still for any such problems not to be very quickly resolved or for them to cause much delay. Don't worry about things which might happen, which are many; prepare for the things which can reasonably be foreseen, which are few – and then forget them all.

8

Cycle-camping

Camping usually conjures up a mental picture of big
trailers behind big cars, frame tents of terrifying
complexity taking half a day to pitch and with which it
would be quite impossible to move on daily, and large
volumes containing addresses of camping sites, studded
with symbols indicating the facilities available at them –
by implication, the more symbols the better the site.

But that is not the image which the cycle-camper sees.
To him, the word camping conveys a unique freedom and
mobility using the simplest of equipment and the
minimum of facilities. It is a free-and-easy, uncomplicated
way of touring, but cycle-camping does not mean
'roughing it'. Few cyclists, once hooked on camping,
would exchange the cosiness of the tent and sleeping bag
in a quiet spot for more conventional accommodation.

Most important from the cycle-camper's point of view
are the weight and bulk of his equipment – it is only
comparatively recently that really lightweight tents and
other equipment of small dimensions when packed have
become widely available and this has led to an increasing
interest in camping by cycle. The complete outfit need
amount to little more than 20 lb. (9 kg) and can be packed
in standard cycle bags.

Several manufacturers, British and continental, offer
tents which, complete with poles and accessories, weigh
about 4 lb. (2 kg) and which pack (without the poles) into
a carrying bag measuring some 12″ × 8″ × 3″ (30 × 20 × 8
cm). Even lighter tents are on the market, but these are
usually skimped in some way, simply to save a few

ounces, and it is false economy – for example, there may be little or no porch to the tent, or the flysheet may not extend down to the ground.

This weight of tent is often listed as 'two-man' but is somewhat cramped when so occupied and there is little or no room inside for anything besides the two men. For solo use such a tent is ideal, however, with ample room for the camper and all his belongings under cover in comfort. Lightweight tents for three or more people are also made, and the weights do not increase in proportion to the space they provide.

Tent poles always have to be carried separately on the cycle and telescopic poles are the most convenient. They take up less room and it may even be found that they will fit neatly into the seat tube of the cycle. This involves removing the saddle pin each time the poles are to be used or put away, but this is worth-while for the neat and thief-proof stowage which results. (There is often a taper on the end of the saddle pin which enters the seat tube,

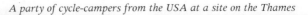

A party of cycle-campers from the USA at a site on the Thames

reducing the diameter of the pin so that it will not take the poles. It is a simple matter to saw off the tapered portion – about $\frac{1}{2}''$ only – of the saddle pin.)

'A' poles for tents are so called because they assemble in the shape of that letter, so giving an unobstructed entrance to the tent. These cannot be carried as suggested.

Alternatively, poles can be strapped to the top of the pannier carrier, or made the last item to be packed in the saddlebag – they will project a little in either case but will not slide about if firmly packed. Some telescopic poles are a close fit, so they should be made perfectly clean before telescoping so that they do not jam and become inseparable when needed again.

Tents are of the simple (central) pole 'bell' type or the two-pole ridge type; the small bell tent has some 4' 6" (127 cm) headroom at the centre and the two-man latter is about 3' 6" (117 cm) high at the front and 1' 6" (45 cm) at the back. Floor area is approximately 4' (122 cm) square in a bell tent and in a ridge tent tapers from roughly 3' (91 cm) at the front to 1' 6" (45 cm) at the rear.

The tents described as 'one-man' are really only suitable for occasional solo fine-weather camping at home, or for summer touring abroad where fine weather can be relied upon, but they have very little spare space and most equipment will have to be left outside suitably protected.

All modern tents have a sewn-in groundsheet. A model should be selected with a groundsheet having a raised section at the front of the tent; this ensures that the outfit is water and insect-proof.

Also recommended is a flysheet which pegs down to the ground all the way round. This is the most effective design to keep wind and rain out, and it has the added advantage that it provides a little extra storage space between tent and flysheet, e.g. at the rear of the tent where the flysheet extends outwards from the inner tent.

The tent should also have at least a small porch – over which the flysheet should also extend – which will be much appreciated for the general ease of circulation which it affords and when cooking in inclement weather.

Proofed cotton is not much used for tents now, and it is in any case heavier, bulkier and less easy to dry than man-made fibres. Polyester-type fabrics, which include Terylene, have advantages over the polyamide ones, which include nylon. They induce less condensation inside the tent (though there will always be a certain amount) and having very little stretching properties are less flappy in wind. Zips should close from bottom to top, allowing control of ventilation at the top of the tent whilst reducing draught.

A filled sleeping bag is essential and there is a wide range on the market. As with everything else, the right

The simplicity and freedom of cycle-camping

advice is to buy the best you can afford, taking into consideration the amount of use to which it is going to be put. Real down (goose or duck) filling cannot be bettered for warmth and comfort coupled with lightness, but natural down is getting scarce and expensive and the latest man-made fillings run it close and are cheaper.

Filled sleeping bags are stitched to form panels to stop the filling wandering about inside; the stitching should be such that it does not form channels in the bag which are without filling and thus form cold strips. Zips on sleeping bags tend to form a cold strip but this is usually at the side of the bag and not serious; a half-length zip down one side of the bag only is sufficient for getting in and out in the confines of a tent.

A good down-filled bag will roll into a 'stuff bag' 8″ in diameter and 12″ long (20×30 cm); bags with other types of filling are fractionally larger when rolled. The weight of either should be between $2\frac{1}{2}$ and 4 lb. ($1\frac{1}{2}$–2 kg).

A sheet sleeping bag of the youth hostel pattern gives added warmth and comfort and helps hygiene, besides having a pillow-case which is useful. Some clothing packed into a stuff bag makes an adequate pillow, though an inflatable plastic cushion is light and a luxury easily carried. Air beds or foam strips, however, begin to make for too bulky a load for the cycle. There is nothing more comfortable to sleep on than hay, if you can find some; otherwise fern fronds make a good substitute. Springy turf is also good. The only discomfort sometimes experienced sleeping on the ground is at the hips, though they get used to it after a few nights and cease to complain. Try putting a little air into your spare inner tube, rolling it and placing it under your hip!

The choice of small stoves for cooking lies between the traditional paraffin pressure primus stove, the similar pressure stove using petrol and the gas cartridge type unit. (There are very simple stoves using only methylated spirits or solid fuel in tablet form, but they are both expensive to run and very limited in the length of time they will burn on one charge; furthermore, the fuels cannot be so widely obtained as to be reliable. These stoves are only suitable for an occasional 'brew-up'.)

Gas cartridge stoves and petrol stoves have recently enjoyed increased popularity in spite of their inherent dangers. They are not cheap to run, and there are signs that in future the two fuels may not be so universally available as hitherto. Either the smallest gas stove or petrol stove will fit neatly into the side pocket of a saddlebag and will last about $1\frac{1}{2}$ hours on one filling – a gas cartridge or two-fifths of a pint (225 ml) of petrol.

The seasoned cycle-camper tends to rely on the hardy paraffin primus stove. The half-pint size gives a good two hours strong burning per filling, and when dismantled occupies only half a saddlebag pocket. The initial cost is quite high, but you need only ever buy one of these stoves as they are so durable.

A nest of small pans for cooking and for use as plates, or a billycan and a couple of plastic plates, plastic cup, and a knife, fork and spoon set complete the vital requirements of the camper. A certain amount of food can be carried in the nested pans or the billy; cut the number of plastic food containers required to a minimum as they are wasteful of space.

For the solo cycle-camper, the tent and all accessories except the poles, and the sleeping bag, will pack into the saddlebag and leave room for other items. One pannier will hold food supplies and cooking equipment and the other the wardrobe. There should always be a little space left for the packing of food purchased on the road, even if this means carrying a small extra bag for this special purpose.

Don't take a lot of things which 'may come in useful'. Take only what will be used. Talk with other cycle campers – each will have his own routine and tips which he will be glad to pass on to you. Certainly, he will tell you what tent he has got and which features led him to choose it.

There are several camp site guides to this country and abroad published here each year, and others are produced in continental countries. They are all aimed at the 'heavyweight' or motor camper or caravanner and the sites listed will be crowded in the summer, although there is usually room for a cyclist and his small tent in a corner somewhere. Fees vary considerably from place to place.

Many cyclists do not find the conditions at such sites congenial, as they are such a contrast to their quiet mode of travel and enjoyment, although some find it useful to patronise one of them now and again when on tour for the occasional luxury of laundry facilities etc. Many of the listed sites are open only for a limited summer season.

It is possible to find camping sites 'away from it all' both in open country or by the kind permission of the farmer or landowner – which should always be sought where necessary. It is rarely refused to the genuine tourist awheel; he should offer to pay – the offer will not always be accepted.

Those going camping abroad should obtain an International Camping Carnet obtainable from the Cyclists' Touring Club for a nominal fee. This is a personal document with international recognition among touring and camping organisations as well as being a guarantee that you are a genuine and responsible camper; it is also an identity document and a useful form of introduction to those from whom you are seeking camping facilities. It includes third-party and equipment insurance.

9

Touring in Europe

Passports
All residents of the United Kingdom must possess a valid
passport for travel to all other countries, except the Irish
Republic. The standard British passport costs £6 and is
valid for ten years. Application forms for passports are
available on request at main post offices, and when
completed must be sent or taken, with the fee and other
necessary documents, to the appropriate regional passport
office, the location of which is given in the notes which
are issued with the application form. Two passport-type
identical photographs are required.

The passport office for the whole of Scotland is in
Glasgow. Northern Ireland residents may take their
applications to the Passport Agency at Belfast (which does
not handle correspondence or postal applications) or post
them to the Glasgow office.

All applications should be made a month before the
passport is needed. Personal attendance at a passport
office does not secure priority treatment. A passport is
usually issued for travel to all foreign countries (but a visa
may be required before some may be entered – see below).

Note that a wife travelling with her husband does not
require a separate passport providing that her name was
included in her husband's passport when it was issued.
A husband may travel alone on such a 'joint' passport,
but not a wife, who must have her own individual
passport to do so.

There is also the 'British Visitor's Passport' costing £3,
which is valid for one year and intended for short holiday

visits to countries in Western Europe. It is not accepted
by all countries. It is a simpler document than the full
passport and can be obtained with little delay through
any main Post Office (not through passport offices) on
submission of the appropriate form properly completed,
the fee and two passport-type photographs.

Parties of juveniles with between five and fifty
members may travel on a 'Collective Certificate' instead of
individual passports. This costs £6 and the adult leader of
the party must have a normal passport of his own. The
London passport office deals with enquiries about this
facility for groups of under-eighteens.

Visas

A few European countries require every visitor to obtain
a visa before admitting them. A visa is a certificate,
usually taking the form of an authenticated rubber stamp
in the passport, issued by the Embassy or Consulate in the
U.K. of the country concerned. It may be an 'entry visa',
permitting the holder to spend a certain length of time in
the country, or a 'transit visa', entitling him to pass

A keen cyclist will take his cycle everywhere!

through the country en route to another.

The regulations concerning visas and the charges for them vary from time to time, so enquiries about the need for them and their cost should be made in good time, either from the Embassy or Consulate concerned or through a travel agent. Before being issued with a 'transit visa' it may be necessary to provide evidence that permission has been granted for entry to the next country, so that any visas wanted should be obtained in the reverse order of visits.

Some countries in eastern Europe (e.g. Rumania, Poland) require some form of advance payment of accommodation costs, usually in the shape of vouchers paid for in London and used in the country concerned for payment at hotels, etc. The grant of a visa to enter these countries is dependent on the production of these vouchers as proof of reservation of accommodation for a minimum period (at least seven days).

The vouchers may cost more than one would otherwise spend. They can be obtained only through the travel agent making the arrangements for the visit and he will normally apply for the visa at the same time.

Currency

There is a limit to the amount of money which may be taken abroad, the amount being fixed annually by the Treasury for the year ending on 31 October. The sum taken is entered in the passport by the issuing bank.

Foreign currency and traveller's cheques may be obtained from any bank for a small fee whether or not one has an account at the bank. They may also be obtained through travel agents but they will require a commission as well as the bank charges which they incur.

Other countries also have limits on the amounts of their own and other currencies which may be imported and exported. In some cases this is nil, all money having to be taken in and out in the form of cheques, so that care must be taken not to have any cash left on leaving the country – paper money (but not coin) can usually be exchanged at an office on the frontier but it is better to budget so that this necessity is avoided. Every change of money incurs payment of a commission by the traveller.

The amounts involved and the number of countries concerned are such that regulations of this kind are not likely to cause great inconvenience, but they are points to be checked before departure. Banks will readily give up-to-date advice and assistance.

The safest way of carrying money is in the form of traveller's cheques. The individual buying them signs them in the presence of the issuing official and countersigns them in the presence of the paying official abroad, so that even if they should unfortunately be lost they are unlikely to be of value to anyone else and their value can be claimed from the issuing bank providing that the loss of the cheques, with their numbers and details of the loss, are promptly reported both to the local police and the issuing bank.

Cash lost is unlikely to be recoverable, but a limited amount of local currency in cash should be taken to meet immediate expenses on arrival and in case of emergency.

Cheques should be cashed at banks abroad. Exchange offices will encash them, as will many hotels, but here again a second commission will be taken to your disadvantage. Remember that banking hours are short and that banks close at weekends and on public holidays (which are more numerous on the continent than at home).

Traveller's cheques are issued in denominations of £2, £5, £10 and £20 or their equivalents. They should if possible be purchased with the value stated in the currency of the country in which they will be used. They will then always be acceptable – there have been occasions when sterling has not been, and travellers have had difficulty in encashing cheques issued for sterling sums. On return to this country, any unused traveller's cheques or paper money (but not coins) may be reconverted into sterling.

Customs
Customs regulations, like exchange rates, vary from country to country, but the cyclist is unlikely to infringe them. Current rules can be ascertained before departure; they are more strict in eastern than western Europe.

On return to the U.K. one may import a few items free of duty and failure to declare anything in excess of these renders one liable to heavy penalties. A list of duty-free items is freely available at ports, airports and travel agencies but in this matter as in all those mentioned in this chapter the cyclists' own travel agency, C.T.C. Travel Ltd., will readily give every help.

If you take a camera, a pair of binoculars or other valuable item out of the country with you, remember to take also the receipt which you obtained for it when you purchased it. This will provide proof that it has not been bought abroad for the Customs officers on your return; equally, it is evidence abroad that it was purchased at home.

Health
The National Health Service does not operate outside the United Kingdom and cyclists travelling abroad are recommended to take out insurance to cover possible medical expenses incurred in other countries. Such expenses can be very heavy.

Most United Kingdom subjects and members of their

families on a temporary visit to other countries in the
European Economic Community are entitled to urgent
medical treatment on the same basis as insured nationals
of the country concerned.

In some other countries in Europe British holiday
visitors are entitled (under the terms of reciprocal
agreements with those countries) to receive medical
benefits on the same basis as nationals of those countries.
These agreements currently exist between the U.K. and
Austria, Bulgaria, Poland, Yugoslavia, Norway and
Sweden.

Eligibility for treatment and its extent, and details of
any documents which must be carried to obtain treatment
if required, should be made the subject of enquiries
before departure as they vary from country to country.

Throughout the continent – the British Isles are no
exception – mosquitos and midges are often very
troublesome and some preparation to prevent or minimise
their attentions should be used. Malarial mosquitoes have
been eliminated from Europe. Adders are found in
Europe but rarely offend; there are species of dangerous
scorpions in the southern and eastern Mediterranean
coastal belts but they are not often encountered – it is as
well, however, not to put an arm or hand into rock
crevices and similar places in these areas.

Enquiries about any vaccinations or inoculations that
may be necessary should be made three months before
travel. They are not often required but special circumstances lead governments to stipulate certain precautions
from time to time, and some treatments take several
weeks to become effective.

Language
You are lucky if you speak English because it is the most
widely spoken language and the most-taught second

language in many foreign countries. In general, the staffs
of big stores, banks and hotels in major cities on the
continent include members who speak English.
Interpreters are available at most major railway stations
and airports.

In Scandinavia and the Netherlands, most of the
population have a working knowledge of English;
elsewhere, except in the most rural areas, it is usually
possible to find someone with at least a smattering if
necessary. Children, many of whom learn English at
school, will be eager to practise their knowledge – more
eager than their elders who will have forgotten most of
what they ever learned and who will be less ready to
converse! All will be found approachable and as helpful
as possible though.

It pays, however, and adds much to the enjoyment of a
holiday, if you know a few words of the language of the
country you are touring, as well as being a courtesy to
your hosts. So get a phrase book and do your best – or
even take a few lessons before you go; the knowledge
will always be of value.

There are a few places with difficult dialects. In Alsace,
eastern France, the everyday language is a French/
German mixture, but almost everyone can speak pure
French and German and will do so if you speak one or the
other to them. The German spoken in northern
Switzerland is very different in accent to standard
German, but here again the people will speak the latter if
you do. Austrian German is different again, but the same
applies.

French is the language of western Switzerland, and
Italian is spoken in southern Switzerland; a small area of
eastern Switzerland has its own language, Romansch,
which is like Welsh in that it is a difficult language
spoken by comparatively few people, and one rarely
learned by foreigners.

In countries occupied by Germany once or more this
century many people, especially the older ones, will have
a good knowledge of German although it is still usually
advisable to make it clear that you are not German even
though you are (having a try at) speaking that language.

Cycling and travel

In all European countries except the British Isles, the rule
of the road is to drive and ride on the right and to
overtake on the left. If night riding is a possibility, try to
fix your lamps on the left-hand side of the cycle. For
night riding, have a red rear lamp and reflector and a
white front lamp, and you will fulfil lighting regulations
everywhere.

Spare parts, tyres, tubes, etc. for British cycles are
occasionally available on the continent, but do not rely
upon being able to obtain them; all spares likely to be
required should be taken on the tour. Ready assistance
with a repair will be given by the staff of cycle shops,
garages, blacksmiths and the like, who are often prepared
to go to some trouble to get a cycle roadworthy again.

If you plan to cycle in the mountains, do not forget
that, even in high summer, it can be cold several
thousand feet above sea level. Although you might keep
warm riding up a pass, it will be chilly when stopping,
and when descending the other side. Take ample clothing
for such conditions.

Tickets for any intermediate journeys by sea, rail or air
on the continent may be purchased before departure
from this country in the same way as the main outward
and return travel tickets. By so purchasing them you
avoid the need to carry extra money with which to buy
them abroad, and the amount they cost does not then
come out of your travel allowance.

Payment for the carriage of cycles, however, must
always be made at the time of registration and cannot be

made in advance. Take care, therefore, to reserve sufficient cash for this purpose on every occasion – including the registration of the cycle back to this country at the end of the tour.

When registering a cycle by rail, insist that the machine be weighed if you can – it is not always possible to persuade station staff to do this.

The cost depends on the weight of the machine and the distance to be travelled, and the estimated weight is invariably higher than the actual weight, resulting in a small overcharge for it. Cycles are not conveyed on 'Trans-European Express' trains.

An appreciable saving in fares is offered by most railway administrations for parties of ten or more travelling together to and from the same destinations. Normally it is worthwhile to pay for ten people if eight or more are so travelling.

It is not easy to generalise about the carriage of cycles on buses on the continent but an indication is given under each country. In some places, buses are equipped to carry a few machines, elsewhere drivers can often be persuaded to take them. As (unlike in Britain) coach travel abroad is very little cheaper than rail, the service is of little interest to cyclists except where there is no railway. Cycles are not accepted on long distance coaches.

The majority of mountain passes are closed by snow during the winter, the impassable period depending on their height and location. Almost all maps of mountain areas show against each pass the dates between which it is open (sometimes there is a separate list at the foot of the map). Road signs showing whether passes are open or closed are placed at the foot of all approach roads.

Many outdoor activity organisations abroad (for skiing, mountaineering, etc.) have chalets and huts in mountain and remote areas where accommodation (and sometimes

food) is provided. These are primarily for their own
members but the occasional intrepid cyclists who reach
such districts are welcomed. Specific enquiries about the
existence of any such organisations should be made to the
appropriate National Tourist Office of the country
concerned. A list of these offices in London is in
appendix 2. They also supply free of charge lists of hotel
and *pension* accommodation and of official camping sites.
General tourist literature about their countries is also
freely available from them. Camping is allowed in the
grounds of many youth hostels (hostel toilet and cooking
facilities may be used) but no generalisation can be made
about the extent of this facility.

All but the roughest of ways and the sheerest of
mountains are accessible to the cyclist. Some cycle
tourists find particular pleasure in finding tracks and
paths that are normally unused; the enjoyment of such
'rough stuff' is an acquired taste and for the benefit of
those wishing to sample it those who have acquired it
have kept records of the routes they have found, both at
home and abroad. The Rough Stuff Fellowship and the
Ordre du Col Dur (see appendix 3) collate these details.

Cycling on canal towing paths is a less adventurous but
very rewarding part of touring. The going is flat, and
canals usually traverse quiet countryside and avoid
towns; even where they do pass through built-up areas
they afford a quiet route and views of the locality which
are rarely seen and often of interest. The British
Waterways Board issues individual permits to cyclists
wishing to use the towpaths of canals under their
jurisdiction where cycling can be allowed. The permits
are issued annually, the fee is modest, and enquiries
should be sent to the Board at Willow Grange, Church
Road, Watford, Herts.

Canals which are not the responsibility of the B.W.B.

are subject to local regulations; signs indicate where cycling is not permitted. Towpaths exist along about 150 miles of the River Thames where cycling is permitted unless notices indicate otherwise. Some other rivers offer similar scope.

Some towpaths are narrow, eroded or ill-kept in places, and on these care – and sometimes a detour – is needed.

Possibilities for towpath riding also exist on the continent but there is no record of local facilities there; it is usual to investigate likely paths 'on the ground' as a tour progresses.

When touring in certain countries, particularly Bulgaria, Czechoslovakia, East Germany, Portugal and Spain, do not loiter in the vicinity of military establishments or 'strategic' points like bridges, dockyards, airfields, railways, etc. Photography is forbidden in

Towpath cycling takes one along very pleasant and unfrequented ways

certain places of this kind, and its prohibition is indicated
by small signs at frequent intervals showing a large cross
over the outline of a camera. Look for them on lamp
standards, fences, etc. Even where this sign is not
displayed, it is unwise to photograph anything other than
the sort of scene a tourist would naturally wish to record.
The authorities are not anxious to interfere with you or
your enjoyment of your tour, but the wishes of the
people in whose country you are a guest should be
observed.

General guidance is given in the following sections on
the travel services to other European countries from
Britain. Services change from time to time and precise
information should be obtained when dates and
destinations of travel are decided. Reference to fares,
costs and exchange rates have been avoided as they are
unstable and quickly go out of date. Current information
about these should similarly be obtained when
requirements are known.

Brief reference is made to a number of areas in each
country in which good cycle tours can be made. The list
is not exhaustive – in fact, it is difficult to think of areas
which do not provide scope for an interesting tour.

10

The countries of Europe

Austria

Getting there
Rail/sea   The direct routes are Folkestone/Calais-Basel,
Dover/Ostend-Luxembourg-Basel and Dover/Ostend-
Munich, the former being the cheapest route to Salzburg
and destinations beyond.
Air   Frequent services by many airlines go from London
(Heathrow and Gatwick) to Vienna and Salzburg. There
are good rail connections to other parts of Austria from
these towns and also from Zurich in Switzerland.

Travelling in Austria
There are local rail and bus services throughout the
country. Cycles can sometimes be conveyed by bus. Rail
and road speeds are modest due to the mountainous
nature of the country. Rail tickets are valid for use on
parallel steamer services on the river Danube on payment
of a small supplement.

   In some mountain areas postal buses are the only means
of public transport. Most of the lakes have steamers
serving the towns and villages on their perimeters; cycles
may be taken on them.

   Internal air services are very few.

Cycling
The use of cycle paths is compulsory. Main roads with
good surfaces follow the river valleys, and many of the
roads over the mountain passes are also wide and smooth;

some, however, and some secondary roads and passes,
have loose surfaces, and are often steep and winding.

Accommodation
There is plenty of accommodation everywhere. As well as
hotels, there are many inns (*Gasthof* and *Gasthaus*), which
are found in even the smallest villages. The former always
provide accommodation but the latter may not always do
so. Rooms to let for a night or longer in private houses are
very common and are indicated by the signs *Zimmer*,
Fremdenzimmer or *Zimmerfrei* (see explanation under
Accommodation in German section).

There are only some thirty youth hostels in Austria,
most of them in the popular resorts and very heavily used
in holiday seasons.

Good but simple meals at reasonable prices can be
obtained at almost all restaurants and inns.

Some touring areas
Salzkammergut   This is the Austrian Lake District,
which is of great beauty but which has the highest
rainfall in the country. The lakes form two chains in the
mountains north of the main Alpine range, these being
the Dachstein group, the Totes Gebirge and the Höllen-
gebirge. There is excellent cycling round the lakes and
some hill climbing in between them.
Vorarlberg and Tirol   The two westernmost provinces
contain some of the finest scenery in a country which is
full of magnificent landscapes. The direct road from the
frontier at Feldkirch to Innsbruck crosses the Arlberg
Pass, 5,911 ft (1,802 m). Between Bludenz and Landeck
the alternative Silvrettastrasse may be taken rising to
6,662 ft. (2,032 m). There are numerous side valleys
worthy of exploration.
Bregenzerwald   A less-frequented area between Dornbirn

and Warth in northern Vorarlberg on the German border.
Forests cover the mountain slopes and Bregenz itself is an
interesting medieval town on Lake Constance.

Carinthia   This is another province of lakes and
mountains in the south-east of Austria, bordering on Italy
and Yugoslavia in the south. The area usually enjoys good
summer weather; the average summer temperature of the
water of the Millstättersee (a lake) is 77°F. (25°C.).

Lower Austria   The easternmost province, differing in
character from the rest of Austria, includes the Vienna
plain and the Danube lowlands. Northwards from the
Danube the land rises towards the Bohemian Forest and
Moravian heights of Czechoslovakia.

Climate
Snow covers the country during January, lasting until
late March in the mountain districts and until late April
above 6,000 ft. (1,830 m). Summer is hot, the south and
east having more sunshine than the west, which also has
more rainfall.

Language
English is understood in large shops, banks, etc., in major
centres, but not elsewhere.

Maps
For route planning: Holzel General Map 1:600,000.
For detailed route finding: Holzel 1:200,000 (four sheets
cover the country).

Belgium and Luxembourg

Getting there
Rail/sea   The direct route via Dover to Ostend is the

obvious choice. Frequent car ferries, which will take
cycles, sail from Dover and Folkstone to Ostend, and from
Dover and Felixstowe to Zeebrugge. There are main line
rail connections at Ostend for Brussels, Luxembourg city
and places en route.

Air   There are frequent scheduled flights from London
(Heathrow) to Brussels and Luxembourg, and an air ferry
service from Southend to Ostend, with rail connections
from London (Liverpool Street) to Southend, and from
Ostend to Bruges, Ghent, Brussels, Louvain and Liège.

Travelling in Belgium and Luxembourg

Belgium has a good railway network with an adequate
and efficient train service. There are special tourist tickets
obtainable locally which show a saving if good use is
made of the trains.

Tramways (cycles not carried) run the whole length of
the coast and also connect many towns and villages
inland. Bus routes operate everywhere. Facilities are
similar in Luxembourg, where the railway system radiates
from the capital, Luxembourg city.

Cycling

Road surfaces in north and west Belgium are often in
poor condition, with large, uneven cobblestones in (and
sometimes several miles each side of) many towns and
villages. Where there is a cycle path (the use of which is
obligatory) the surface is usually superior. In eastern
Belgium and Luxembourg road surfaces are better and
where cobbles are encountered they are usually evenly
laid and present no problems for the cyclist.

Cycles must be fitted with a bell.

Accommodation

Both countries are well provided with hotels and
pensions. In Belgium there are two youth hostels

associations, the Flemish (in the north) and Walloon (in the south). There is a good coverage of hostels, those in the north being larger and more formal than those in the south. Luxembourg has a number of well-sited hostels.

There are plenty of restaurants, but the popular café does not serve food, only coffee, minerals, beers and ices.
Special Note   The Belgian and Luxembourg franc are of equal value, i.e. they are tied to the same exchange rate. Belgian money is accepted in Luxembourg, *but Luxembourgois currency cannot be spent in Belgium*.

Some touring areas
Western Belgium   Belgium is a compact and heavily populated country. Large towns and industries are few, but much of the country is intensely cultivated and hence thickly settled. Typical of this is the Plain of Flanders, in the two coastal provinces of East and West Flanders.

This flat area has no dramatic scenery but is of general interest and includes several notable medieval towns, chief of which are Bruges and Ghent. It is also noted for its art galleries and museums.

Numerous minor roads offer a good choice of cycling from Ostend to Brussels, visiting these places of interest on the way.
Northern Belgium   The provinces of Antwerp and Limburg are less fertile, with much heathland and bog. Nevertheless there is much pleasant riding between Ghent or Brussels and Antwerp, and thence to Louvain and Liège, with frequent sightseeing spots.
Eastern Belgium and Luxembourg   The hills of the Ardennes extend southeastwards of a line joining Liège, Namur and Charleroi into northern Luxembourg. This is an area of great scenic attraction and an excellent choice for a first cycle tour abroad.

The wooded, rounded hills rise to no more than 2,200

ft. (670 m); the roads do not climb as high as this and
have very good surfaces. Near Dinant are the famous
grottoes of Rochefort and Han – the latter being 10,000 ft.
(3,050 m) long and containing a huge cavern, a lake and
an underground river. On production of their current
membership cards, C.T.C. members are admitted at
reduced prices.

Central and southern Luxembourg is a continuation of
the Lorraine scarpland which is an average of 400 ft.
(120 m) lower than the Ardennes. There are many old
towns, usually with an ancient castle perched on a high
point, creating the 'fairy-tale' atmosphere always
associated with this small country.

Climate
The climate is similar to that of southern England but it is
slightly colder in winter and warmer in summer. Fogs
often occur in the west. Rainfall increases towards the
southeast of Belgium where the Ardennes rise, but
decreases again in Luxembourg, in the shelter of the same
hills.

Language
In northern Belgium, Flemish (very similar to Dutch) is
spoken, and in the south French. Many places have both
a Flemish and a French version of their names and many
street names are exhibited in both languages. Public
servants everywhere normally speak both languages.
There is a small German-speaking minority near the
German border at Eupen.

The people of Luxembourg are tri-lingual, speaking
Luxembourgian as the everyday language. The written
languages are everywhere French and German, the former
being the language of the law courts and government and
the latter the language of the newspapers. Everyone
speaks both, and English is widely known also.

Maps
For route planning: A.I.T. 1:500,000 (Belgium,
Luxembourg and the Netherlands on one sheet).
For detailed route finding: Michelin 1:200,000 (four
sheets cover the countries).

Bulgaria

Getting there
Rail/sea   There is a daily service from London
(Victoria) via Dover/Calais-Paris (change termini)-Milan-
Trieste-Belgrade-Sofia, with through carriages from Paris
to Istanbul. Departure from London is in the early
afternoon, and Sofia is reached in the evening of the
third day. Alternative routes are London (Victoria) via
Dover/Ostend–Cologne–Munich–Salzburg–Zagreb–Sofia,
and London (Liverpool Street) via Harwich/Hook of
Holland–Cologne, then the same route to Sofia. Journey
times are similar to the first route, and on both a change
of train is necessary in Munich.
Air   There is a daily direct flight from London
(Heathrow) to Sofia.

Travelling in Bulgaria
Main railway lines radiate from Sofia to adjacent
countries, serving the main Bulgarian centres en route. A
few branch lines in the east of the country complete the
system. Trains are slow and the rolling stock elderly.
Regular bus services connect all towns and most villages.
Do not loiter in the vicinity of military or strategic
installations, or attempt to take photographs of these or
industrial complexes. Remember to respect the Bulgarians'
way of life.

Cycling
The main road from the Yugoslav frontier at Dimitrovgrad
to Sofia, Plovdiv and the Turkish frontier has been
designated a motorway and no provision appears to have
been made for other road users. Visiting cycle tourists are
known to use this road, riding on the roadside path which
extends for varying distances along its length. Other main
roads radiate from Sofia to southern Yugoslavia (Skopje),
to Rumania and to the Black Sea coast. All these roads are
busy. The minor road system gives access to all regions of
the country but surfaces are generally poor; slow
progress is being made to improve them. Streets in towns
are often cobbled.

Accommodation
Tourists and all visitors from abroad must stay at the
state-appointed hotels, guest houses or camp sites. The
country is quite well provided with these but in popular
districts (main towns, Black Sea resorts) booking in
advance – or a start to the search for accommodation
during the afternoon – is advisable. Restaurants and cafés
are not common outside the capital and the popular
districts and in general the diet is adequate but plain
except in the highest class of hotel.

Some touring areas
The Danube and the Balkan Range   For 300 miles (480
km) the Danube forms the frontier between Bulgaria and
Rumania in the north; parallel with it east to west and
some 70 miles to the south is the ridge of the Stara
Planina, or Balkan range of mountains with several peaks
well over 6,200 ft. (2,000 m). The area is a platform rather
than a plain, and there are often high cliffs overlooking
the Danube where it abruptly ends. There is good
mountain scenery, especially the Isker gorge south of

Mezdra, and there are some towns of historic interest, though many are affected by the modern industrial development which is common in Bulgaria.

The Rose Valley   Parallel to and south of the Stara Planina is a lower hill range, the valley between the ranges containing 'Rose Valley', a very extensive rose-growing area of outstanding beauty in May and early June. The road through the valley is the shortest route between Sofia and Bourgas, a Black Sea resort, and is often busy.

The Black Sea Coast   There are numerous resorts which tend to spoil Bulgaria's only coastline. Former palaces and aristocratic villas have been converted into holiday houses and stand alongside modern tourist hotels. Access to some beaches is restricted; others are very crowded in summer. Some resorts are of entirely modern creation. The road does not hug the coast all the way but a good tour can be made combining coast and the hinterland which is alternately wooded, farming and fruit-growing land.

The South-West   Here are the highest mountains in the country, with Moussala rising to 9,650 ft. (2,925 m), extensive apple orchards, forests and (in the far south-west) tobacco plantations. There are few roads, but sufficient to make a circular tour of a striking area.

The South   Here the Rodop mountains dominate forests. Some of the numerous valleys have good roads which serve mining districts and power stations (with their associated traffic) but which give access to much scenic beauty as well.

Climate

In the north, summers are hot, with periodic thunder-storms, and winters cold, with winds from the north-east. South of the Stara Planina, it is somewhat less disturbed; summer is longer, and winter a little less cold. The far

south is warmest all the year round and here, unlike the
rest of the country, most of the rainfall is in winter.

Language
Very few people speak English.

Maps
Maps are very difficult to obtain anywhere. A good atlas
gives the best impression of the country; route planning
and finding must normally be based on road diagrams
produced for motorists. In some areas the best touring is
by a succession of side trips off a through road.

Cyprus

Getting there
By sea   The island is served by a number of passenger
and passenger-carrying cargo lines from ports in the
Aegean, Mediterranean and North Sea (including Britain),
the voyage taking up to twelve days, dependent upon
departure point.
Air   Direct flights leave London (Heathrow) daily for
Nicosia, and there are many connecting flights from other
main cities of Europe.

Travelling in Cyprus
There are no railways, but buses connect all the towns
and villages. The cyclist is unlikely to need public
transport in Cyprus, which is 125 miles × 50 miles
(200 km × 80 km) in size.

Cycling
Two-lane surfaced roads radiate from Nicosia to the main
inland and coastal towns, and there is a good network of

single-lane surfaced roads which covers almost all of the
island except for the western part of the Troodos
mountains. This area and all others are served by narrow
roads with loose surfaces. All roads tend to be somewhat
bumpy but all can be ridden comfortably. Cycle shops
and mechanics are to be found in all large towns.

Accommodation
There are hotels in all major towns and in many villages;
the former are very well-appointed, the latter often
simple; prices reflect the difference. There are several
youth hostels – in Nicosia and in the western part of the
island (the east can be explored from Nicosia). The
climate is ideal for camping; confirmation of the
possibility and propriety of camping should be obtained
for any site thought suitable.

Touring
Two mountain ranges cover much of the island. The
Kyrenia mountains in the north have some fine quiet
roads. The larger and higher range, the Troodos
mountains in the west, have very many winding roads
and tracks through banana, citrus and palm groves to the
upper pine forested areas. Between them lies the fertile
Messoria plain. Everywhere the countryside is good, and
everywhere there is much of historic interest.

Climate
Summers are very hot and dry: skies are cloudless and
streams dry up. The winter is mild in the plains and in
the coastal belt (340 days of bright sunshine annually) but
colder in the mountains, where there is snow from
January to early April.

Language
Greek is spoken by 80% of the people, almost all the rest

speaking Turkish. English is widely spoken.

Map
Survey of Cyprus Administration and Road Map, the
official State map, 1:250,000. Excellent for all purposes.

Czechoslovakia

Getting there
Rail/sea   There is a daily service from London (Victoria)
via Dover/Ostend–Cologne–Passau–Vienna (change of
train necessary)–Prague. Less direct and less convenient
services run via Dover/Calais or Boulogne–Paris (cross
between termini)–Strasbourg–Stuttgart, and via Harwich/
Hook of Holland–Venlo–Cologne–Nurnberg (change of
train)–Prague.
Air   There are frequent flights from London (Heathrow)
to Prague.

Travelling in Czechoslovakia
Main line railways run through the country from east to
west (U.S.S.R. to West Germany) and cross the country
from north to south from Poland and East Germany to
Vienna. There is also a main line from Prague to Budapest.
The few branch lines complete an adequate rail system.
Supplements are payable on main line trains except for
holders of tickets issued outside the country.
   Local and long-distance buses cover the country but
cycles are not normally carried.
   Do not loiter in the vicinity of military or strategic
establishments, or attempt to take photographs of these or
of industrial complexes.

Cycling
There is a comprehensive system of major and minor

roads. Traffic is light except on the major roads between
main centres (Plzen, Prague, Brno) and those entering
from the east. Surfaces are good. There are cycle shops in
most towns where repairs can be carried out, but spares
should be taken.

Accommodation
There are about a dozen youth hostels, widely spaced and
mainly in the west and north. Hotels and restaurants are
plentiful.

Some touring areas
The country is naturally divided into two main areas by
the river Morava, which flows from north to south
roughly down the middle of it.
The West is the more thickly populated and has the
better communications. The interesting capital city of
Prague is centrally situated. Southward lies Bohemia,
with very attractive wooded hills and valleys, and the
Bohmer Wald mountains which form the frontier; the
whole region is very hilly, the northern part rising to the
Erzgebirge and Sudet Peaks at the frontier.
The East   Splendid Carpathian mountain scenery
dominates in the north, including part of the High Tatra
range (shared with Poland). Parts of the region are
among the most densely wooded in Europe. Many old
villages and crafts survive but much modern industry is
being superimposed.
The Southern Plain   The valleys of the Morava and
Danube (which forms the frontier with Hungary) make a
small, pastoral region centred on Bratislava. This area can
be included in a tour of either or both of the others.

Climate
This varies with local relief and aspect; the higher parts

of the frontier mountains receive 40″ (1,000 mm) of rainfall annually, the sheltered lower areas half that amount. Average winter temperatures are freezing everywhere; in July the lowlands average is about 67°F. (19°C.) the rest of the country being progressively cooler as height is gained.

Language
The western part of the country is Czech, the east Slovak. They speak almost identical languages.

Maps
For all purposes: Freytag & Berndt 1:600,000 (one sheet covers the country).

Denmark

Getting there
Rail/sea   London (Liverpool Street)–Harwich/Hook of Holland–Hamburg–Copenhagen, twice daily. London (Liverpool Street)–Harwich/Esbjerg–Copenhagen: daily in summer, three times a week at other times of the year. London (Kings Cross)–Newcastle/Esbjerg–Copenhagen: summer only, three times a fortnight on variable days. Boats from Newcastle leave from Tyne Commission Quay, nine miles from the railway station. There is no provision for the carriage of cycles on the connecting buses between these points but cyclists may take the local train from Newcastle Central to Percy Main which is about a mile from Tyne Commission Quay.
Air   Frequent flights go from London (Heathrow) to Copenhagen, and a few from Glasgow and Manchester to Copenhagen.

Travelling in Denmark
There is a good service of trains on the countrywide
railway system. A special visitor's 'season ticket' offers an
advantageous rate if good use is to be made of the
railway; it is also valid on buses and internal ferries. The
principal ferry services are between Nyborg (Funen) and
Korsør (Zealand), Copenhagen and Arhus, Alborg (Jutland)
and Rønne (Bornholm), and Hundersted (Zealand) and
Grena (Jutland).

Cycles are carried on all except local trains. They
should be registered the day before travel to ensure they
arrive in time (this does not apply to Esbjerg–Copenhagen
trains). Buses do not convey cycles.

Cycling
Away from towns, main road surfaces are excellent and
minor road surfaces good. In towns the roads are often
cobbled. In general, roads are straight and take gradients
'in their stride' rather than following the contours.
Cycling is allowed everywhere in woods and nature parks
belonging to the state. In private woods and parks which
exceed 9 acres (5 hectares) in size, cycling is allowed
between dawn and dusk on existing roads and tracks.
Cycles must be locked when left unattended.

Many bicycles are in use in Denmark; there is a mass
exodus from the towns to the sea and country at
weekends.

Accommodation
A good youth hostel system exists, the hostels being very
well equipped. ('Family' rooms can be booked for two or
more cyclists.) Hotels run by the Y.M.C.A. are very
suitable for touring cyclists. 'Bed and Breakfast' houses
similar to those in Britain can be found near towns and
holiday places during the summer.

Meals in restaurants are enormous but expensive.
Cafés with the sign *madkurve kan medbringes* (own food
can be brought) are useful. Note that camping is allowed
away from the listed sites either by permission of the
owner of private land or on public land except where
there is a notice *Teltslagning Forbudt* or *Ingen Camping*.

Some touring areas
There are no mountains in Denmark but it is a very
undulating country even though there are no hills higher
than 500 ft. (152 m). The country consists of the Jutland
peninsula (bordering on West Germany), the two large
islands of Funen and Zealand, and 500 small islands.
Water crossings by ferry and bridges are therefore
features of any cycle tour in the country.
Jutland (Jylland)   The west and north is mainly flat with
large wild areas of sand and heather. Some of the smaller
roads are gravel surfaced. The central part is hilly and
contains an attractive 'Lake District' with towns and
villages nestling in the valleys. The coast in the eastern
part has many fjords. In the south a pastoral landscape
typifies the agricultural nature of the country,
particularly dairy farming.
Funen (Fyn)   Called the 'Garden of Denmark', this is an
island of pretty villages, manor houses, woods and lakes.
Zealand (Sjaelland)   The largest island is a 1½-hour boat
crossing from Funen. The best touring areas are in the
centre and north, which has extensive woods, lakes and
interesting towns. A fine road runs along the north coast,
called the 'Danish Riviera'. Copenhagen stands on the
east coast of Zealand.
Bornholm   A week could well be spent on this lovely
island, although the road round the coast is only 90 miles
(145 km) and much can be seen in a shorter visit. The
boat from Copenhagen takes seven hours; another way to

get there is to cross to Malmö (Sweden) from Copenhagen ($1\frac{1}{2}$ hrs), cycle the 40 miles (64 km) to Ystad, thence take the ferry to the island ($2\frac{1}{2}$ hrs). Good cliff scenery, houses for smoking herrings, and famous round fortress-churches are among the many interesting features.

Climate
The Danish climate is similar to the English, but with greater extremes. The mean temperature in January and February is freezing point and July is the warmest month with an average of 60°F. (16°C.). Rainfall is least in spring and heaviest in late summer and autumn. The prevailing winds are westerly.

Language
Most Danes have a good knowledge of English, German, French and Swedish.

Maps
For route planning: Tourist Map of Denmark 1 : 500,000. For detailed route finding: G.I. 1 : 300,000 (three sheets cover the country).

Finland

Getting there
Rail/sea   The following route takes about 35 hours: London (Liverpool Street)–Harwich/Hook of Holland– through carriage to Copenhagen, then an overnight rail journey to Stockholm, steamer to the port of Turku and rail to Helsinki. It is also possible to travel via London (Victoria)–Dover/Ostend–Brussels–Aachen–Bremen– Copenhagen, thence to Helsinki as above. Cycles are

registered to Copenhagen from London, then payment
and registration are necessary for each separate section of
the onward journey. (Note that Customs examination
takes place at Harwich and not London on the Hook of
Holland route.)

Air   There are daily flights between London (Heathrow)
and Helsinki.

Sea   Regular but infrequent sailings from Tilbury to
Helsinki take $3\frac{1}{2}$ days, normally calling at Copenhagen
and Gothenburg en route (and sailing on to Leningrad).
There are also regular sailings to Helsinki from a number
of North German ports, and direct sailings from
Copenhagen.

Travelling in Finland

Railways cover most of the country except Lapland, as do
bus services, on which cycles may be taken. There are
also extensive lake steamer services. Tourist travel tickets
are available which give a choice of areas and which may
be used on the three means of transport. Internal air
services operate between Helsinki and the chief provincial
towns.

Cycling

There is an extensive road system in the southern half of
the country, with good surfaces. The few main roads into
the northern part are also well surfaced but in the north
most roads are minor and often stony.

Accommodation

There are many youth hostels, mostly small and open
only for the months of June, July and August. The south
and west of the country is adequately supplied with
hotels and *pensions*, but the north, where habitations are
often few and far between, is sparsely covered. Tourist

inns exist in the main centres. Good meals at reasonable prices are obtainable at smaller restaurants and coffee bars.

Some touring areas
A circular tour from Helsinki can embrace much of the coastal plain in the south (there are hundreds of off-shore islands), the upland plateau behind, and many lakes (there are over 50,000 lakes in Finland). The gradients here are not severe. Towns en route are Turku, former capital of the country, Tampere, through which the Tammerkoski Falls pass, Jyvasklya, set in wild scenery, and Savonlinna, where plays and folk dances are held in the old castle in summer. The area is thickly forested.
Lapland   A region of scrubland and higher fells and moors reaching to over 4,000 ft. (1,240 m). In the north-west there is a National Park (Pallastunturi). Rovaniemi lies in the Arctic Circle and is the capital of Finnish Lapland.

Climate
The winter is long and severe, icebound but mostly dry. Rain for long periods is rare, the annual total being only 21" (53 cm). The summer is short but warm; Helsinki is warmer than London in July which, with August, is the best period for cycling in Finland.

Language
In the chief cities, many people speak English.

Maps
Hallweg 1 : 1,000,000 is adequate for all purposes.

France

Getting there

Rail/sea   There are four daily through rail/sea services
between London and Paris (including the night ferry) all
the year round – two via Folkestone/Calais, one via
Newhaven/Dieppe (the cheapest route but the longest sea
crossing) and one via Dover/Dunkerque (the night ferry).
These services are augmented during the summer months.
The same applies from Paris to London. British and
French railways operate a number of car ferries which are
most suitable for cyclists making port-to-port journeys.
Cycles may be wheeled on and off these. Privately
operated car ferries are Townsend/Thorensen Ferries
(Dover/Calais and Southampton/le Havre or Cherbourg)
and Normandy Ferries (Southampton/le Havre) and these
take passengers without cars. Cycles may be wheeled on
and off these.

Hovercraft   Several crossings are operated daily by
British Rail (Seaspeed) between Dover/Boulogne/Calais
and by Hoverlloyd between Ramsgate/Calais. There is a
special concession for members of the Cyclists' Touring
Club wishing to travel with their cycles on British Rail's
Seaspeed hovercraft from Dover between April and
September, when cycles are not normally accepted. They
may do so by booking through C.T.C. Travel Ltd. or on
production of their C.T.C. membership cards at the
Seaspeed counter, Eastern Docks, Dover when booking
there. These services are affected by bad weather conditions and when these prevail passengers are sometimes
transferred to ordinary ships.

Air   Many international airlines operate between
London (Heathrow and Gatwick) and provincial airports
to Paris and Nice, giving a very wide choice of departure
times every day of the week. British Air Ferries fly

Southend/le Touquet and London/Paris via Southend/le
Touquet (air) with rail connections London/Southend and
le Touquet/Paris.

Travelling in France
French Railways offer a modern, fast and punctual
service. Some major centres (e.g. Lyon) have a service of
regular fast trains from Paris throughout the day, but the
general scheme of things is that expresses leave Paris for
the provincial towns and resorts – inland and coastal –
and for destinations beyond the frontiers of France late at
night and early/mid-morning. Day and night services
respectively from London connect with these trains,
time being allowed to cross between arrival and
departure termini in Paris. The cyclist should ride
between the terminal stations; the only other way to do
it is to walk. A street plan of the city, freely available
from the French Tourist Office, will show how to avoid
the main traffic intersections en route.

   All long-distance night trains have sleeper accommodation as well as seats. Sleepers vary from the simple (and
cheapest) *couchette* (six per compartment, blanket and
pillow provided) to second-class sleepers (four per
compartment) and first-class (privacy with a proper bed
and individual washing facilities). Seat and sleeper
reservations both to Paris and from Paris to other
destinations can be made in London, early application
being essential. For those spending at least five days in
France and travelling (or paying for) at least 1,500 km of
rail travel in the country, a special tourist fare applies
which shows a reduction of 20% on the normal fare.
There are some very fast trains which are first-class only,
often with a supplementary charge, operating mainly to
the south and south-west of France – to be avoided if the
budget is tight. Some do not convey cycles.

Many local bus services operate in France and on most
of them cycles may be carried on the roof.

Air France operate internal services between major
centres, e.g. Paris to Biarritz, Nice, Marseilles, Strasbourg.

Cycling
Where cycle paths are provided, their use is obligatory.
As well as the international cycle-path sign, they may be
indicated by a notice *Piste Cyclable Obligatoire*. Riding
two abreast is permitted but riders are expected to go
singly in towns and when traffic conditions make it
advisable. Almost all drivers sound their horns when
about to overtake and usually give cyclists a wide berth
when doing so.

It is compulsory to use an orange or white front lamp
and a red rear lamp when riding at night *or when visibility
is bad*.

All roads shown on Michelin maps are suitable for
cycling. The 'N' roads are the trunk routes carrying
heavy traffic but they can almost always be avoided. The
'D' roads and the unnumbered roads (uncoloured on the
maps) have good surfaces and are quiet and enjoyable for
cycling. In some towns, especially in northern France,
many roads are cobbled. Care is needed on these at all
times. Signposting everywhere is excellent. Hub gears are
unknown in France and dynamo cycle lighting universal.
Spares for these gears and front lamp batteries are
therefore unobtainable.

Accommodation
There is little or no private accommodation in France of
the 'bed and breakfast' type, but there is a very large
number of hotels of all sizes and grades. Every town of
any size has a number of hotels. Those in the side roads
are cheaper, quieter and more homely than those on the

main streets. Hotels in fashionable resorts and at the
summits of mountain passes are invariably expensive.
Inns in the *Logis de France* group offer good accommodation at reasonable prices. A list of them is available from
the French Tourist Office.

The country is very well provided with restaurants at
which good food freshly cooked can be obtained at any
hour of the day, every day of the week. The *Relais
Routiers* is a chain of restaurants displaying a distinctive
sign; they provide substantial meals at reasonable prices.
All the main touring centres have an office called the
Syndicat d'Initiative, often open till late evening; these
have complete information about local accommodation
and are always pleased to help find the kind required.
Youth hostels at which Y.H.A. membership cards are
valid are mostly to be found in the tourist areas with few
in between, but there are several organisations in France
which run chains of similar establishments going under
the general name of *Auberge de la Jeunesse* (Youth Hostel).
If seeking this kind of accommodation, simply enquire for
the *Auberge de la Jeunesse*. With these, as with all other
kinds of accommodation, it is normal practice to have a
look at the facilities offered before accepting them.

Official camp sites abound in France. An inclusive fee
is charged at each site depending on length of stay and
covering the use of the toilet, laundry and other facilities
provided. Camping elsewhere is permitted and in the wild
areas of the country splendid isolated sites are easily
found. Permission should be sought before camping on
private property.

Some touring areas
France is a large country – three times the size of Britain –
and has the greatest variety of landscape of any country
in Europe. All parts are full of interest and offer great

scope for the cycle tourist.

North of Paris lies the most industrialised and thickly populated region, with low hills, plains and farms, and little in the way of natural scenery. A network of minor roads facilitates quiet exploration, which can be undertaken from one of the channel ports, possibly on the way to a more distant part of the country.

Normandy is also easily reached from England, to which its scenery is similar: hilly but not mountainous, with farms, orchards and woodland and long sections of coast having sheer cliffs down to the sea. A 'comfortable' countryside, with small ports and villages and the typically unhurried way of life of rural France, it is a good area for a first tour abroad.

The Loire Valley is similar but more spacious. Famed for its *châteaux*, of which there are well over a hundred between Gien and Angers. Quiet minor roads offer alternatives to the busy tourist routes even in the high season, but for proper appreciation of the *châteaux* a visit out-of-season is best.

Alsace/Lorraine   Alternate possession by France and Germany over the centuries has produced a difficult local dialect but almost all residents speak both languages. This area of eastern France includes the Vosges mountains, a splendid wooded range with rounded summits at 3,500–4,500 ft. (1,065–1,370 m).

The Alps   Within France lies a section of this tremendous mountain range some 250 miles long and up to 80 miles across, stretching from the Mediterranean coast to the Lake of Geneva, and culminating in Mont Blanc, 15,782 ft. (4,812 m). Alpine flowers and chalets in the north, stone farmhouses and lavender in the central section, and arid hillsides with clustering villages in the south are connected by many high passes. These average some 6,000 ft. (1,830 m) above sea level at their summits but

occasionally reach 8–9,000 ft. (2,440–2,705 m).

Côte d'Azur   The 'French Riviera', drawing many visitors with its predictably fine climate, is between Marseilles and Menton on the Mediterranean coast. Much of this coast is spoiled by crowds of people, motor traffic, advertising and excessively high prices. A few quiet spots remain, but the cyclist will prefer to tour in the much more placid and interesting hinterland of Provence, making visits to points on the coast rather than riding along it.

The Rhone Valley is the obvious approach route to the Côte d'Azur but is a main artery for traffic by road, boat and rail. For much of the way through the valley a quieter road on the west bank of the river is an alternative to the main highway on the east bank. Avignon, Arles, Tarascon and Montélimar are among the very historic places in the valley. Attractive side trips into the hills on either side of the valley are recommended.

The *mistral* is a north-westerly wind which blows from central France down the Rhone valley to the sea. Most frequent in winter, it can occur at any time and in summer, even when the sky is cloudless, it is quite cool. It gathers strength as it blows towards the Rhone delta. It is a help to cyclists riding southwards but the reverse if heading upstream.

Massif Central   A very large area in south central France with a great variety of scenery, ranging from numerous extinct volcanoes at the centre to forests, broad meadows and dramatic scree-covered hillsides further out.

The Pyrenees   A mountain range nearly 300 miles (480 km) long dividing France from Spain. An almost complete

Most of Europe has a network of minor roads which are ideal for cycle tourists

lack of public transport and of petrol stations on all
except the low-level roads leaves the well-surfaced minor
roads through the hills devoid of unsightly development
and free for the cycle tourist. There are many fine passes
of 5,000 ft. (1,525 m) or so, the highest being the Port
d'Envalira (on the border of the tiny state of Andorra) at
7,900 ft. (2,410 m).

Corsica   This island is agreed by the great majority of
cycle tourists who have been there to be the perfect
touring ground. Lacking in museums and galleries and in
major architectural works, Corsica offers instead great
natural beauty, a wealth of small villages and a glorious
coastline. Narrow but with fair surfaces, the winding
hilly roads (which see a minimal amount of traffic) enable
the island to be fully explored by the cyclist. The climate
is hot and sunny throughout the summer, malaria and

Summer sunshine in Corsica

bandits no longer exist, and apart from a few developing resorts (e.g. Calvi, Propriano) and holiday camps on the east coast, the island remains unspoiled.

Corsica is reached by air from Nice or Marseilles. Summer boat services operate from Toulon, Nice and Marseilles to Calvi, Ile Rousse, Bastia, Ajaccio and Propriano. Services are most frequent in August (up to four sailings a day) but are at irregular times. The summer sailing schedule is available from E. H. Mundy & Co. (Passenger Agencies) Ltd., 87 Jermyn Street, London, S.W.1 early in the year and bookings should be made in good time for travel in the holiday season.

Climate
In the north, the climate is similar to that of southern England, but it is a little warmer and drier. In the east, there are greater extremes, with warmer summers and colder winters, and it is somewhat wetter in summer than in winter. In the south-east (Cote d'Azur) summers are hot and dry, and winters mild. In the south-west, summers are warm but often wet, and winters are mild. In the west, Atlantic conditions prevail, with winds all the year round, stormy wet periods in summer and cool damp winters.

Language
English is understood in large shops, banks, etc., in Paris and in the south of France resorts, but not often else-where.

Maps
For route planning: Michelin 1:1,000,000 France, or Bartholomews 16 miles to 1″ (two sheets: Northern France and Low Countries, and Southern France). For detailed route finding: Michelin sectional maps

1:200,000 (35 sheets cover the whole of France; all of
Corsica is on one sheet).
Michelin 1:100,000 (environs of Paris).

Andorra
This is a small republic in the eastern Pyrenees between
France and Spain. It consists of gorges and valleys and is
surrounded by high mountains. Its area is 191 square
miles (49,470 hectares); the language is Catalan, but
French and Spanish are spoken and both currencies
accepted. The only road through between France and
Spain crosses the Port d'Envalira, 7,900 ft. high (2,410 m).

Monaco
A small principality on the French Mediterranean coast
between Menton and Nice, Monaco has an area of 368
acres (149 hectares) and is a highly developed holiday and
gaming resort. There are some interesting buildings (e.g.
the palace in the old town, and the aquarium). French is
spoken and French currency used.

Germany (East)

Getting there
A visa is needed for entry into East Germany (the German
Democratic Republic), the issue of which is dependent
upon the possession of vouchers for accommodation for
all the nights it is intended to stay in the country; refer
to page 84. The vouchers are issued for specific hotels or

camping sites and must be paid for in advance; confirmation of bookings accompanies them and these papers must be submitted with passport and payment so that a visa can be issued.

If for any reason it is not possible to obtain a visa before leaving Britain, it will be issued on the train at the frontier crossing point upon production of the above documents and on payment of the fee.

Exit visas are granted at the same time as entry visas and are free of charge.

The usual entry point from Britain is Helmstedt, on the route (daily service) from London via Dover/Ostend to Brussels–Cologne–Hannover–Magdeburg (and *West* Berlin). Other rail entry points are Bebra (between Frankfurt/Main and Leipzig), Probstzella (between Nürnberg and Leipzig), Hof (between Munich and Dresden) and Karl-Marx-Stadt (between Vienna/Prague and Dresden). There are at present no direct flights from Britain to airports in East Germany.

Travelling in East Germany
There is a good internal rail network, and trams and local buses in all towns. Services are reliable, if not high-speed.

Accommodation
There are hotels in a large number of cities and towns, and camping sites in the vicinity of many of them as well as in regions of scenic beauty. There are a number of youth hostels in town and country – for which vouchers and confirmation of bookings must be obtained in advance as described above – which are open to everyone under the age of 30; a youth hostel membership card is not required. Most hotels, restaurants and shops will accept payment in foreign currency.

Touring in East Germany
It is not possible to make a cycle tour in the usual sense in East Germany. Cycling is confined to the areas immediately surrounding the centres at which accommodation has been pre-booked; travel between centres is by train, so that a few small 'centre tours' only may be made.

Historic cities and centres of the arts include Berlin, Dresden, Potsdam, Weimar and Leipzig; whilst attractive scenic areas include the valleys and lakes of Thuringia, the Harz mountains and the mountains of Saxony, and the tideless Baltic Sea coast with white, sandy beaches.

Photography is unrestricted except for military establishments and railway installations.

Climate
Summers are warmer than in Britain (in the eighties Fahrenheit, 30°C.) and winters colder with heavy snowfall.

Maps
For route planning: R.V. 1:500,000 (one sheet covers the country).

For detailed route finding: V.E.B.L.V. 1:200,000 (official survey, nine sheets cover the country).

Note that in view of the limited possibilities for cycle touring in East Germany, these maps are not essential.

Local town guides and plans are sufficient and are obtainable from the National Tourist Office in London and local tourist offices in East Germany.

Germany (West)

Getting there
Rail/sea   The cheapest and shortest route is via
Dover/Ostend and Brussels to the Belgo/German frontier
at Aachen, from where there are rail connections to most
parts of the country. For destinations in northern
Germany, however, the Harwich/Hook of Holland
crossing is often more convenient and certainly more
comfortable. Note that Customs clearance of cycles takes
place at the port (Harwich) and not at the London
departure station (Liverpool Street).
Air   Frequent air services are operated between London
and Cologne, Frankfurt, Munich and other main cities.

Travelling in Germany
German railways are efficient and punctual. Express
trains are very fast and local trains very slow. On many
express trains a supplement is payable unless a through
ticket issued abroad is held. Tickets issued abroad permit
an unlimited number of breaks in the journey, whilst
with tickets issued in Germany this number is limited.
Buses connecting with the trains are operated by the
railway administration.

   Where there are no railways, the Post Office provides
the bus services with yellow vehicles which are a
common sight and which serve even the remotest
mountain villages. Some long-distance services operate in
tourist districts. There is accommodation for a few cycles
in many cases but the availability of this facility where
desired should be checked in advance.

   Steamer services operate on Lake Constance and the
river Rhine. Fast boats navigate the Rhine as well as the
ordinary service and these are more expensive to use.
Rail tickets are valid on parallel boat services on the

payment of a small supplement. On the Rhine and Mosel and other rivers there are ferries at various points by which passengers and cycles may cross cheaply. (These are marked with an 'F' on maps.)

Lufthansa operate internal services between major cities, e.g. Hamburg, Cologne, Munich, Frankfurt.

Cycling

Few cycle paths exist, but where they do, their use is compulsory. Riding two abreast is illegal but is tolerated on quiet minor roads; the police have absolute authority to instruct single file riding.

For internal rail journeys in Germany with a bicycle, a bicycle ticket must be purchased (the cost is modest and depends on the length of the journey) and the cycle must be loaded and unloaded by the passenger.

Most road surfaces are generally good, but cobbled streets still exist in many towns and villages, and in some towns tramlines are very awkwardly placed from the cyclist's point of view.

Accommodation

The youth hostel system in Germany is huge, with many hostels in all parts of the country except the south, where they are much thinner on the ground. In Bavaria they may be used only by persons under 25 years of age, except for leaders of parties.

Other types of accommodation are easily found in Germany, where inns (*Gasthof* and *Gasthaus*) abound. These offer a good standard of service and good food at reasonable prices. The country is also well provided with hotels of superior grades, and very many private houses exhibit a *Zimmer* notice, especially in the south of the country. This indicates that there are rooms to let for one or more nights, but food is not normally provided; food may be taken in, or meals taken at a nearby restaurant, of which there are also plenty. At these houses the room is invariably spotlessly clean and very comfortable, and full toilet facilities are available for the use of guests. The charges are very reasonable.

The usual accommodation lists are obtainable from the German Tourist Information Bureau in London but of all places Germany is the one where you may most confidently travel without worrying about booking ahead or about having difficulty in finding accommodation.

Tourist offices (*Verkehrsamt*) are found in most towns, often open till late evening, where the staff are ready to assist with finding rooms. Official well-equipped camp sites are numerous throughout the country. Camping elsewhere is allowed but permission should be sought.

Touring in Germany

The northern part of West Germany is known as the Northern Lowlands, or North German Plain, and is comparatively flat farming country with marshes and heathland. It includes two large industrial conurbations – the maritime cities of the north-east and the Ruhr in the south-west.

Further south are the Central Uplands, low ranges of hills divided by many rivers. There is a good deal of industry of wide variety.

Southernmost of all is the Alpine Foreland, a high plain rising to the Alps, of which only a narrow strip lies within Germany.

The North   The area between the frontiers of the Netherlands, Denmark and the East German Republic is the least interesting part of the country from the scenic point of view but it is ideal for those who like to get off the beaten track and see places rarely visited by tourists. There is much of architectural interest, much flat farmland, and much opportunity to see and mix with the local people. Lüneburg Heath, the Tuetoburg Forest, the Weser hill country, part of the Harz mountains (which extend into East Germany), the Sauerland, part of the Rhine valley and the Eifel are all in this district.

The middle Rhine Valley   The Rhine valley has much in common with the Rhone valley in France, being a busy traffic artery for rail, road and water-borne passengers and freight, with alternative quieter roads in some parts and the possibility of interesting side trips into the hills at either side.

Between Koblenz and Bingen is the Rhine Gorge, where the river winds for 40 miles between steep hillsides. Ruined castles adorn the hills, which are covered with vineyards. At Koblenz the Rhine is joined by the Mosel, another valley well worth exploring.

The Bavarian Forest   South of the frontier between West Germany and Czechoslovakia is a thickly forested area extending to the Danube. It is thinly populated and rarely visited by tourists, and old customs, folklore and festivals are still practised.

The Spessart adjoins the Forest to the south and contains many towns unchanged – apart from traffic – since the Middle Ages, among them Rothenburg ob der Tauber, Dinkelsbühl and Nördlingen. It is an area of beautiful countryside which extends into the next Bavarian district of *Schwaben*, with its towns of Munich and Augsburg and further rolling, wooded countryside up to the Austrian and Swiss borders.

The Black Forest (Schwarzwald) is about 100 miles (160 km) long and situated between Pforzheim and the Swiss frontier in the south-west of the country. (It is easily reached from Alsace in eastern France.) It is characterised by abrupt hills rising to 3–4,000 ft. (1,015–1,320 m) with equally abrupt climbs and descents on the

roads, and by patches of pine forest with rolling meadow-
land in between.

The Bavarian Alps are integral with the Austrian Alps
and both may be conveniently visited in the course of a
tour. They can however be traversed on the German side
between Lindau (Lake Constance) and Bad Reichenhall
either entirely by road (a devious but interesting trip) or
with the use of some stretches of path and track for those
who do not mind some mild 'rough stuff'.

Climate
It is more settled than the English climate, with colder
winters and warmer summers, the extremes of heat and
cold widening the further east and south one gets.
Afternoon heat in the south in summer can be oppressive
and violent thunderstorms sometimes occur.

Language
English is understood in large shops, banks, etc. in main
centres but not elsewhere.

Maps
For route planning: Michelin 1:1,000,000 (Germany and
Northern Europe). For detailed route finding: Mairs
(Stuttgart) Generalkarte 1:200,000 (26 sheets cover the
whole of W. Germany); Michelin 1:200,000 (the only
parts of W. Germany covered by this series are
Dusseldorf/Rhine Valley, Eifel/Mosel Valley, Frankfurt/
Rhine Valley, Black Forest, Stuttgart/Ulm).

Note
West Berlin is accessible by air without formality; there
are frequent daily flights from London (Heathrow). For
overland travel to West Berlin, a transit visa for the
German Democratic Republic (East Germany) is needed.

It can be obtained in advance from the GDR Embassy or through a travel agent on payment of the appropriate sum, or it will be issued on the train at the frontier crossing point on payment of the fee and production of passport.

There is a daily service by rail/sea from London (Victoria)–Dover/Ostend–Brussels–Cologne–Hannover–Helmstedt (frontier station)–Berlin, and a nightly service from London (Liverpool Street)–Harwich/Hook of Holland–Amersfoort–Osnabrück–Hannover–Helmstedt–Berlin.

Other entry routes are:
(Copenhagen)–Warnemünde–Rostock–Berlin
Hamburg–Buchen–Berlin
Frankfurt/Main–Bebra–Leipzig–Berlin
Nürnberg–Leipzig–Berlin
Munich–Hof–Dresden–Berlin
Vienna/Prague–Dresden–Berlin

Greece

Getting there
Rail/sea   The journey from London (Victoria) to Athens via Folkestone/Calais–Milan–Belgrade takes nearly four days. Following the same route as far as Salonika takes nearly $3\frac{1}{2}$ days. Cycles are handled throughout these rail journeys by railway staffs and must be registered to their rail destination; owners have no access to them en route.

Car ferries run between Brindisi (Italy) and Igoumenitsa on the west coast of Greece, Corfu and Piraeus (the port of Athens).

Other approaches by sea are from Venice, Genoa and Marseilles to Piraeus.

Air   There are daily flights between London (Heathrow)
and Athens and Salonika.

Travelling in Greece
A good system of rail and bus services covers the
country. Cycles can be taken by bus. Travel tickets
should be purchased locally in advance to avoid long
delays at booking offices.

Cycling
Main roads are well surfaced and often busy; minor roads
are usually in poor condition. A spare tyre and tube
should be carried as well as the usual tool kit. There are
one or two cycle shops/repairers in Athens but few, if
any, elsewhere.

Accommodation
There is a good youth hostel network. Hotel
accommodation is plentiful and private accommodation
can usually be found on enquiry to the tourist police or
at local cafés. There are official camp sites but camping is
permitted almost everywhere.

In restaurants it is usual to visit the kitchen to choose
the dish desired.

Some touring areas
From Athens to Delphi is a distance of 100 miles, through
wooded hills that gradually become mountains. At Delphi
there are many imposing classical ruins and an interesting
museum.

The Peloponnesus   This peninsula forming the southern
part of Greece is joined to the mainland by the isthmus of
Corinth, four miles wide. Mountains rise to 8,000 ft.
(2,440 m) and among them are small plains and valleys,
some with little or no vegetation and some green with

olive groves. Impressive remains of ancient civilisations
abound.

The Northern Provinces   In the north there are charming
villages and mountain ranges, with much evidence of
earlier Turkish times. Fortresses and monasteries,
churches and towns, all of antiquity, provide great
variety over small distances. The Tempe Valley, Mount
Olympus, Jannina, Salonika and the peninsula of
Chalcidice are among the places of outstanding interest.

The Islands   Of the many islands of Greece served by
boats from Piraeus, those of Crete, Rhodes and Corfu
(Kerkyra) are large enough to warrant taking a bicycle for
exploration; Crete is by far the largest, being 140 miles
long.

Climate
Summers are dry and hot, with little or no rain, except in
the mountains of the north. Winters are mild, with the
heaviest rainfall on the west coast and the western and
northern mountains. The lowlands in the Salonika region
sometimes get cold winter spells which spread from the
Balkans.

Language
English is fairly widely spoken.

Maps
For all purposes: Freytag & Berndt 1:600,000 (one sheet
covers the country).

Hungary

Getting there
Rail/sea   There is a daily service from London

(Victoria) via Dover/Ostend–Brussels–Cologne–Nürnberg–
Vienna–Budapest (28 hour journey) and from London
(Liverpool Street) via Harwich/Hook of Holland–Cologne–
Nürnberg–Vienna–Budapest (34 hours). On both routes a
change of train at Cologne is necessary.

Air   There is a daily direct flight from London
(Heathrow) to Budapest. Other daily services involve a
change of aircraft at Paris, or elsewhere.

Travelling in Hungary

A main railway line crosses the country from Vienna
(Austria) via Budapest to Lvov (U.S.S.R.) and Bucharest
(Rumania), and another from Prague (Czechoslovakia) via
Budapest to Belgrade (Yugoslavia). Minor lines radiate
from Budapest to the main centres in all other parts of the
country but there are very few interconnecting provincial
lines. Bus services are limited and crowded.

Cycling

There is a good network of roads, few of which carry an
appreciable amount of traffic. Surfaces are generally
tolerable, but some country roads are unsurfaced and the
surfaces of others have not received attention for a long
time.

Accommodation

There are various grades of state hotels, and enough of
them to enable the whole country to be visited. Camping
is officially restricted to appointed sites.

Some touring areas

The Central Range   So named when the territory of
Hungary was more extensive, these mountains run from
south-west to north-east across the northern part of
present-day Hungary. They are split by the Danube

Gorge north of Budapest, and at their southern end are flanked by the 45 mile (72 km) long Lake Balaton, which is very shallow (13 ft. or 4 m deep) and has wide beaches on the south shore which are used as a summer resort by Hungarian and foreign holidaymakers. It is a pleasant cycling area. As elsewhere, old country towns are becoming centres of industry, but much of interest remains.

The Great Plain   This area of eastern Hungary has much variety. There are sandy plateaux, tracts of loess (a thick, silty deposit), flood plains and reclaimed swampland where rice is grown. It is quiet and undramatic but pleasant touring.

The South-West   The region between Lake Balaton and the Danube is not unlike the Great Plain but is higher and more undulating. The frontier in the south follows the river Drava for some 40 miles, with Yugoslavia on the other side.

Climate
The highest rainfall is in May, June and July, with somewhat more in the west than in the east. In winter the whole country freezes, but summers are very warm.

Language
Very little English is spoken anywhere.

Maps
Maps are virtually unobtainable and recourse must be had to a combination of atlas, guide book and imagination.

Iceland

Getting there
By Sea   There is no satisfactory service. Irregular cargo
boats carry a few passengers, usually at fares higher than
those by air, including a service from Felixstowe via
Hamburg to Reykjavik (a week's voyage). For practical
purposes, boat services are extinct.
By Air   Several flights operate weekly from London via
Glasgow to Reykjavik, but almost all flights advertised to
land at Reykjavik in fact land at Keflavik airport, 30
miles away. A bus for Reykjavik meets each plane but the
carriage of cycles on it is not guaranteed; there is also a
regular bus service between the two towns and the same
applies. If all fails, the ride is on a metalled road.

Travelling in Iceland
There are no railways. Irregular boat services cover most
inhabited parts of the coast except in the south; there is a
charge for cycles on the boats. On buses, cycles are
usually carried free though occasionally a small charge is
made. There are bus services most days in summer from
Reykjavik to Husavik (in the north-east), Olafsvik (in the
west) and Gullfoss (in the south), and two or three times
weekly in some other areas. Bus timetables for the whole
country are sold at Reykjavik Post Office and at the
country bus terminal in Reykjavik, and a current copy
should be consulted. Internal air services radiating from
Reykjavik are good.

Cycling
Only the Reykjavik–Keflavik and Reykjavik–Selfoss roads
are surfaced (and short stretches in townships). The
surface is a metalled strip in the centre – good cycling
when there is little traffic but at other times the cyclist

has no choice but to use the dirt strips at the sides.

Elsewhere, in inhabited country, road surfaces vary greatly from place to place and from time to time but are rarely unrideable; in uninhabited areas many roads cannot be ridden as they are soft, sandy tracks, and some ford rivers at points needing special vehicles or equipment for crossing.

Cycles and gears must therefore be well tested to stand up to the conditions. All spares likely to be needed should be taken, including plenty of tyre canvas. There are very few cycle shops in Iceland and they carry only limited stocks; however, major repairs such as welding can often be arranged.

On the road, pedestrians have absolute priority over turning vehicles, and on roundabouts the inside (right-hand) lane should only be used if taking the first exit, otherwise take the outside lane until the exit is reached.

Accommodation
Hotels are expensive and do not cover the whole country. There are three or four youth hostels, located in the north and the south-west. Accommodation in schools, community centres, etc. in townships is sometimes available for those with their own filled sleeping bags or similar equipment – the word for such accommodation is *svefnpokaplas* and it is always worth enquiring for it in townships. Touring is much restricted unless one camps; there are a few official camp sites with basic facilities.

All townships of fifty people or more have a shop, and there are also a few isolated shops. A cyclist can get to a shop every day for long distances on many roads (but emphatically not on others) providing the location of shops is known in advance so that they can be reached during opening hours.

Some touring areas
In many parts of Iceland there is only one road, so one
rides on it for several days and then retraces it.
Rewarding areas other than those mentioned here cannot
be reached from Reykjavik in a two-week tour unless
motor assistance is available.

The mid-Western Peninsula   Snæfellsnes offers a great
variety of landscape and coastline, and several passes
(open all the year) can be included in a circuit. On the
return, between late June and August when the road is
open, a crossing of the high plateau of Kaldidalur could
be included.

'Fjallabaksleid' is the name of the road through the wild
and uninhabited region north of the southern ice-caps
and for much of its length it is smooth and hard-packed.
It is passable from mid-July and five days should be
allowed for the crossing between Galtalækur (the last
farm on the western side) through Landmannalaugar to
Buland (the first farm on the eastern side) and to the first
shop at Vik i Myrdal or Kirkjubæjarklaustur. It is
advisable to avoid weekends on this road.

The South and West is the main farming area of Iceland;
there are lakes (including the largest, Thingvallavatn, and
a warm-water one, Laugarvatn), waterfalls and glaciers.
The coast road from Vik to the Oræfi mountain area is
now open; Oræfi can also be reached from the west by
plane.

Climate
For the latitude, winters are fairly mild, though severe by
our standards, and summers are cool, but there are
regional variations. In the interior snow can fall at any
time. Rainfall is highest along the south and south-west
coasts but brilliant sunshine is frequent, and high winds

can occur in any month. From June to the end of August is the only practical cycle-touring season; June is perhaps the best time when the chance of rain is less and daylight is at its longest (24 hours a day).

Language
English is widely spoken in towns, but elsewhere few people speak it except for priests, doctors and schoolmasters – though it is always worth trying.

Maps
For route planning: Ferdafelag Islands 1:750,000 (covers the country in one sheet, but note that some 'roads' shown are suitable only for specially adapted motor vehicles and are out of the question for cycling. Map revised 1974).

Surveys of 1902–1939 with revisions 1:250,000 (nine sheets cover the country).

For detailed route finding: 1:100,000 series (87 sheets cover the country).

Note
Iceland has very few places with normal tourists' and travellers' amenities and is a country for the adventure-some and self-reliant cycle tourist with stamina and the ability to cope with all conditions, for whom a visit is a rewarding and worthwhile experience. Prospective visitors to Iceland are recommended to seek the detailed advice of the specialist on Icelandic travel, Dick Phillips, Whitehall House, Nenthead, Alston, Cumbria (between May and October, at Fljotsdal, Fljotshlio, Rang., Iceland).

Irish Republic

Getting there
By Sea   There are sailings from Liverpool to Dublin
(nightly), and from Holyhead to Dun Laoghaire, near
Dublin (nightly, with an additional day service in
summer), from Fishguard to Rosslare (daily and three to
five nights weekly), and from Swansea to Cork (five
nights weekly). There are rail services to all the departure
ports from many parts of Britain, but some will necessitate
a change of train en route. Boat services are heavily used
in the summer and early booking is essential.
Air   Services are operated from London, Birmingham,
Bristol, Cardiff, Blackpool, Liverpool, Manchester,
Leeds/Bradford, Glasgow, Edinburgh and the Isle of Man
to Dublin, and from London to Shannon (near
Limerick). There are also summer services from Luton,
Derby, Exeter and Newcastle-upon-Tyne.

Travelling in Ireland
The rail system links some large towns but there are few
branch lines. There is a frequent bus service in the
Dublin area but elsewhere services are infrequent. Cycles
are carried on the roof. Very few long distance road or
rail services operate on Sundays. There are internal air
services between Dublin and Cork and Shannon.

Cycling
Ireland is ideal for cycling as all roads with very few
exceptions (e.g. Dublin–Cork) have very light traffic even
in summer, and all of them, save a few minor roads in the
west, are well surfaced.

Accommodation
There are youth hostel chains in the Dublin environs

(Wicklow mountains) and in the south-west, but few
elsewhere. They are often small and simple. Bed and
breakfast accommodation is very plentiful everywhere
and is of a high but homely standard.

*At the Black Lake, near the start of the crossing of the Gap of
Dunloe in Killarney, Ireland*

The Irish way of life includes little 'eating out' and apart from in a few large towns small restaurants and cafés are rare. Cycle tourists should have picnic meals during the day.

Special Note
Irish and British currency are of the same denominations and of equal value. British money is accepted in Ireland, but *Irish money cannot be spent in Great Britain or Northern Ireland.*

Some touring areas
Donegal   A wild area, with an impressive coastline; at Slieva League there is a sheer cliff of 1,970 ft. (600 m) falling into the Atlantic and there is much other fine cliff and mountain scenery.
Connemara   An area of bare, rounded hills with a coastline whose good beaches are often deserted except at weekends. Many people here still speak Erse. The Joyce Country, Loughs Mask and Corrib, and Galway are nearby.
The South-West   Cork is the gateway to the south-west. It is a bustling centre with tranquil corners. Cork and Kerry counties have the highest mountains in Ireland, rising to 3,414 ft. (1,040 m), and the famous beauty spot of Killarney. There are many quiet peninsulas extending into the Atlantic in the far south-west which are worth exploring.
The Wicklow Mountains   A small but very scenic range south of Dublin. The valley of Glendalough is a 'beauty spot' and there are many others in the heather-covered hills.

Climate
This is mild, moist and changeable. Rainfall in the east is

much the same as in southern England, about 30″ (76 cm) annually, but it increases towards the west to 80″ (203 cm), being very subject to depressions from the Atlantic. Fine, warm spells occur in summer though they cannot be predicted in advance.

Language
English is in common use, though in certain areas (the remote south and west, and Co. Donegal) the people are Irish (Erse) speaking, and efforts to preserve the Irish language have also led to a good knowledge of it else-where. Some road signs in the remote areas are in Irish but their meaning is obvious.

Maps
For all purposes: Bartholomews $\frac{1}{4}″$ = 1 mile, 1:250,000 (five sheets cover the country).

   (There are $\frac{1}{2}″$ to 1 mile – about 1:130,000 – maps published by the Ordnance Survey of the Republic of Ireland. Twenty-five sheets cover the country. They are not easy to obtain and many are not up-to-date.)

Italy

Getting there
Rail/sea   Most areas of the country are best reached by the service from London (Victoria)–Folkestone/Calais or Boulogne – through train to Milan or Rome via Switzer-land. For Turin, Genoa and the Italian Riviera the preferable route is via Paris, cycling between railway termini, and Modane. Through trains run from Paris to these western Italian destinations, and to Rome on both routes. The fares are the same on the Calais/Boulogne route as on the services via Calais/Lille/Basel, or

Dover/Ostend/Brussels/Luxembourg/Basel, via the Swiss frontier at Vallorbe, Les Verrieres and Delle and the Italian frontier at Iselle instead of Chiasso. Tickets are normally issued for use on any of the routes so return tickets may be used for travel out one way and back another. There are services to all parts of Italy via London (Liverpool Street) – Harwich/Hook of Holland–Germany–Basel, and (for north and north-eastern Italy) via Hook of Holland–Munich–Innsbruck.

Sicily is served by regular boat sailings between Naples and Palermo, and between Cagliari (Sardinia) and Palermo. Other sailings call irregularly from various Mediterranean ports (islands and mainland). There is also a ferry across the Straits of Messina from Reggio Calabria to Messina. Air services operate from Rome and Naples, connecting with flights to and from London.

Sardinia is served by boat sailings between Naples/Civitavecchia and Olbia/Cagliari/Porto Torres and Genoa, and between Cagliari and Palermo (Sicily – see above). Other sailings call irregularly as in Sicily. There is a frequent service on the half-hour crossing between Bonifacio (Corsica) and Santa Teresa Gallura.

Air   Direct flights from London (Heathrow) operate to several major cities from which flights connect to smaller towns.

Travelling in Italy

A countrywide rail network offers the fastest and cheapest means of internal travel. Seat reservations in trains are advised as they are often overcrowded. Cycle charges are rather expensive and the minimum is often higher than the passenger fare for journeys of less than 62 miles (100 km).

There are long-distance and local bus services on which cycles are carried.

Cycling
Main roads everywhere are very busy; in particular the
roads linking major cities and towns in the north should
be avoided. There are alternative minor roads which are
far superior for cycling. Road surfaces are in general good
but deteriorate progressively towards the south. Car
drivers invariably sound their horns at least once when
overtaking.

Accommodation
Youth hostels are more numerous in the north than in the
south. North of Naples and Pescara (Adriatic coast) there
is an abundance of hotel and *pension* accommodation of
all grades. Although this thins out to the south it is
adequate everywhere; however, pressure on
accommodation is very heavy during the long summer
holiday season. Between May and September it is possible
to sleep out in the lowlands; a down bag is advisable but
not always essential. *Trattorie* are local restaurants
varying in character with the district. *Bottiglierie* are bars
where, provided wine is ordered, one may eat one's own
food using the cutlery and plate provided. Cafés usually
serve only coffee, minerals and ices.

Some touring areas
From the Alps to the 'toe' of Italy the peninsula is about
600 miles long. The coastline totals 4,500 miles. There is
great diversity of climate and physical characteristics, and
no other country has so many cities of major cultural
interest.
　　Any of the following regions fully merit exploration
and can well occupy a holiday tour of two or three
weeks' cycling.
Aiosta and Piedmont　　The Alpine region bordering
France and Switzerland.

Western Riviera   The Mediterranean coast between Ventimiglia and Genoa. The resorts are sophisticated but there is some fine coastal scenery and the background of Ligurian hills is worthy of a visit. The coast road is busy but somewhat relieved by a parallel motorway for through traffic.

The Lake District   Lakes Como, Garda and Maggiore are set in the southern foothills of the Alps in central northern Italy.

Venice and the Dolomites   A visit to the city of canals, where there is much of artistic and architectural interest, can be combined with a tour of the Dolomite Alps to the north. Quite unlike the rest of the Alpine range, these limestone mountains look grey, yellow or red with changes of light, and sheer peaks rise abruptly from meadows and forests in dramatic fashion.

Siena, Pisa and Florence   The 'fine art' cities set in the Tuscan countryside.

Perugia and Assisi   Historic cities of Umbria, in the rolling countryside of the central Appenines.

Rome and the Vatican City   Unquestionably the finest city in the world, Rome has not escaped the depredations of modern traffic but remains a magnificent city requiring a week or more for proper appreciation.

The Marches and the Abruzzi   Wild mountain scenery in the Abruzzi National Park and the highest mountains of the Appenines, culminating in the Corno Grande, 9,554 ft. (2,912 m) high.

The South   A remote and primitive area extending from Naples to the 'toe' and 'heel' of Italy.

Sicily   A mountainous and, in summer, arid island where villages do not straggle but sit tightly on hilltops and the coast. The active volcano Etna (11,000 ft.–3,355 m) dominates the south of Sicily, which is the largest Mediterranean island.

Sardinia   Also mountainous and often barren. *Nuraghi*,
fortified dwellings of the Bronze Age, survive in large
numbers and are a common feature of the landscape.
Banditry still occurs from time to time in the Nuoro/
Orgosolo district.

Climate

The south is much hotter than the north, with long dry
periods in summer when day temperatures reach the
nineties (38°C.) in the shade and higher (50°C.) in the sun.
The northern plain is cool in winter and warm in summer
(80°F. or 28°C.), as are the Mediterranean and Adriatic
coasts. Rainfall varies between 30″ (76 cm) annually in
the lowlands to 50″ (127 cm) and more in the mountains,
much of it falling in February and March.

Language

French is the language of the Alpine districts of the Val
d'Aosta and Val Pellice, and German is spoken in parts of
the Trentino. Few people understand English.

Maps

For route planning: Kummerley and Fry 1:500,000 (two
sheets cover the country, including Sicily and Sardinia).
    For detailed route finding: Touring Club Italiano
1:200,000 (24 sheets).

San Marino

This independent republic is 12 miles (19 km) south-west
of Rimini. Bounded by Italian territory, San Marino has
an area of 22½ square miles (6,000 hectares). Italian is
spoken and Italian currency used.

Vatican City State

An independent sovereign state in the heart of Rome, the Vatican City has an area of 109 acres (44 hectares) and consists of the Vatican Palace, the official residence of the Pope, and the basilica and square of St. Peter's. Several other basilicas in and near Rome, and the Pope's summer residence at Castel Gandolfo, are also part of the State. Italian is spoken, and Italian currency used.

Malta

Getting there
Rail/sea   There is a daily service from London (Victoria) via Dover/Calais–Paris–Modane–Rome (change trains)–Syracuse, then a boat to Malta. Boats from various Mediterranean and Aegean ports serve the island.
Air   There are several flights from London (Heathrow) daily, direct or via Rome.

General
Malta is 17 miles by 9 miles (27 × 14 km) in size. It is low-lying and largely agricultural but has much of historical interest; there is a good network of well-surfaced roads. Accommodation is limited and can be difficult to obtain in the summer months, and opportunities for camping are very slight as the land is so intensively cultivated English currency is often accepted and English is understood everywhere.

In summer the weather is hot and in winter very mild. Heavy clothing is not required at any time of the year.

The neighbouring island of Gozo is 9 miles by 4 miles (14 × 6·5 km) and is reached from Malta by a ferry which runs several times a day.

The most useful map is the 1:10,000 Ordnance Survey sheet.

The Netherlands

Getting there
Rail/sea   The direct route is from London (Liverpool Street) via Harwich to the Hook of Holland, from which port there are connecting trains to Amsterdam, the Hague and Rotterdam. It is cheaper and quicker from London (Victoria) via Dover to Ostend, which is only a 25 mile (40 km) ride from the Netherlands border. There are also boat services from Hull and Felixstowe to Rotterdam, and from Immingham Docks to Amsterdam. Bookings for these should be made several months in advance.
Air   There is a frequent vehicle ferry from Southend to Rotterdam and frequent scheduled flights from London (Heathrow and Gatwick) to Amsterdam and Rotterdam. Certain flights operate direct from Manchester, Birmingham and Glasgow.

Travelling in the Netherlands
An electrified railway system serves the whole country. Few places are more than an hour's journey apart by rail. There are no long-distance bus routes, but frequent buses run between neighbouring towns. They do not normally carry cycles; in any case, the distances are hardly worth it.

Cycling
The use of cycle paths is compulsory. There are many of them alongside roads, and some have their own traffic

signals which allow for the slow speed of the bicycle.
There are also many cycleways which are independent of
the roads, giving access to woods and parks and
providing quiet through routes away from other traffic.
Surfaces are good; some roads are cobbled but the setts
are usually smoothly laid.

Cycles must be fitted with a bell, and must be locked
when left unattended.

Accommodation
The country is well supplied with youth hostels and
hotels and there is little difficulty in finding accommodation without booking ahead. Dutch restaurants are a cross
between cafés and public houses. Eating in these is
expensive but most towns have cafeterias where prices
are reasonable.

Some touring areas
The Netherlands is a small, densely populated country
with little open countryside, but it does not lack interest
and most of it can be seen in the course of a two-week
cycling tour. It is mostly flat but the roads often wind.
The Bulb Fields   These are in the Haarlem district and the
flowers are in bloom between mid-April and the end of
May.
The Best Scenery   This is to be found in the Venlo–
Maastricht area of Limburg province, the Eindhoven area
of Brabant, the Arnhem area and National Parks of
Gelderland, Overijssel (Ewolle) and Drente (Meppel).
The Zuider Zee   An interesting little tour round the
Zuider Zee (Ijssel Meer) includes the great enclosure dyke,
the Isle of Marken, where decorated houses are built on
wooden piles, and the people wear picturesque national
dress. Alkmaar's famous cheese market (Friday
mornings) and the fishing village of Volendam can also
be seen.

Fording the stream

Everywhere there are many things to attract the cycle tourist: ancient towns, picturesque villages, architecture and canals among them.

Climate
Very similar to that of south-east England. Winds prevail from the west and they are especially noticeable as the flat country does nothing to temper them. The weather tends to be damp but rainfall is not excessive.

Language
English is widely spoken.

Maps
For all purposes: Michelin 1:200,000 (three sheets cover the country).

Norway

Getting there
Rail/Sea   In summer, Bergen Line boats sail five times a week between Newcastle and Bergen (19 hours) and once a week between Newcastle and Stavanger (17 hours). Sailings at other times of the year are less frequent but cheaper fares are offered for round trips at these times, and for parties of twelve or more on summer services. The Fred Olsen Line operates regular sailings all the year round between Newcastle and Oslo (36 hours), supplemented in summer by a service between Harwich and Kristiansand (22 hours). Cycles may be taken on all these services. The latest time for embarkation is half-an-hour before sailing time.

Newcastle can be reached by rail from many parts of

the country, but there is no provision on the connecting buses for the carriage of cycles for the nine miles between the station and Tyne Commission Quay from which the boats leave. Cyclists must therefore allow time to ride this distance or travel by local train from Newcastle Central to Percy Main which is one mile from Tyne Commission Quay. Harwich is best reached by rail via London, except for those travellers who can conveniently pick up a train at Colchester.

The Bergen Line and Fred Olsen Line sailings *may* leave from Hull instead of Newcastle from 1976.

The shortest other practicable surface route to Norway is via Harwich, Hook of Holland and Copenhagen. The journey takes 36 hours, is expensive and involves at least one change of train en route.

Air   Many of the principal air lines operate daily flights from London (Heathrow) to Oslo, Stavanger and Bergen. It is sometimes necessary to change in Oslo for Stavanger and Bergen.

Boat and air services to Norway are always very heavily booked and it is advisable to apply for reservations at least six months before the date of travel, and even then to give a second choice of date in case the first is already fully booked.

Travelling in Norway

Main line railways radiate from Oslo to Stavanger (in the south-west), Bergen (in the west) and Bodø (in the north), and into Sweden. There are a few branch lines. Trains are not very fast due to the geography of the country and the fact that many of them make 10–15 minute stops at certain stations to give passengers an opportunity of obtaining refreshments.

Buses operate on most principal routes in summer and will carry cycles.

A comprehensive service of coastal steamers and ferries

serves the many ports and villages in the western fjords.
Within the fjords, local boats and ferries connect the
villages with one another and with the ports at the
mouths of the fjords. Faster boats connect the important
villages with the ports or direct with Bergen, capital of
the fjord country. Cyclists arriving at Bergen are thus
enabled to sail to any fjord to start their tour, to use these
shipping services to link different sections of a tour, or to
sail to Bergen at the end of a tour if departing from there.
Winter services are considerably curtailed.

Careful planning is needed with the aid of the boat
timetables (available from the Norwegian Tourist Office)
or the Norwegian *Rutebok*. This is published monthly and
contains a complete timetable of the regular public
transport services (train, boat, bus, ferry) in the country.
On sale at all bookstalls in Norway, it can also be
obtained from B.A.S. Ltd., 22 St. Giles High Street,
London W.C.2.

Internal air services operate daily between Oslo and
Stavanger, Bergen, Bodø and Tromsø.

Cycling
No roads in Norway carry heavy traffic so all offer
pleasant riding. In the southern half of the country main
roads have a metalled surface, but minor roads there, and
all roads in the northern half, are generally unsurfaced.
These are often dusty and tend to get rutted in wet
weather. The dust, dry or wet, is caught up in the chain
and gear mechanism which it is essential to clean from
time to time. It is advisable to take spare spokes as well as
all the usual spares and tools, and a spare chain too if the
visit is to be an extended one. Norway is a very hilly
country, but road gradients (with a few notable exceptions) rarely exceed 1 in 10 thanks to the use of tunnels,
hairpin bends and spirals by the road engineers.

The Norwegian cattle grid (*ferist*) consists of small logs

spaced up to 6" (15 cm) apart and should be negotiated with care.

Accommodation
Youth hostels are of excellent standards. Hotels are very good but expensive. Guest houses (*pensjonats* or *gjestgjiveries*) are less expensive and more homely. Accommodation possibilities and shops are fewer and farther between the further north one goes; they can be 20 miles and more apart, so advance planning is necessary. Norwegians eat well, the food being simple and wholesome. Little beer, wines and spirits are drunk and they are expensive.

There are many official camping sites throughout the country. Camping elsewhere is allowed but permission should be sought.

Some touring areas
The Western Fjords   A typical fjord has a few islands at its mouth, where the sides slope gently upwards, becoming steeper as the fjord cuts its way into the heart of the mountains until at the head they loom over a narrow inlet. The large number of fjords contribute to the length of Norway's coastline which is no less than 21,000 miles (33,600 km). The western fjords extend from Stavanger to Trondheim.

In a generally spectacular region, the following roads deserve special mention for their grandeur:
   The road from Stalheim to Gudvangen along the
      Naeroy Gorge.
   The Mabodalen mountain road and Vøringfoss
      waterfall on the route from the eastern extremity of
      the Hardangerfjord (Eidfjord) to Geilo.
   The Takagjelet gorge east of Norheimsund on the
      Hardangerfjord, where the spectacular views are

visible only from the cycle path which does not tunnel as the road does.

The 'Troll' road, a mountain road between Andalsnes and Valldal.

The 'Eagle' road, a mountain road between Eidsdal and Geiranger.

The road from Geiranger to Lorn with a detour to the summit of Dalsnibba mountain.

The ferry journeys along the Naeroy fjord from Gudvangen to Kaupanger, and along the Geiranger fjord between Geiranger and Hellesylt, are also exceptionally fine.

The South Coast   The coast from Stavanger to Tønsberg and the west side of Oslo fjord is unbroken by inlets or fjords and has many resorts and bathing beaches often sheltered by islands. Unlike the rest of Norway, the countryside behind is of rolling, tree-clad hills which are neither high nor steep.

The Eastern Valleys   These are the five river valleys running north and west from Oslo fjord deep inland. The valley floors are wide, with a lake here and there, and have steep, forested sides. The valley roads climb steadily but not steeply to open moorland; there are several roads over to the western fjords and the heads of the valleys are joined by mountain roads.

The North   North of Trondheim there is a single road winding 1,000 miles to Hammerfest, the most northerly town in the world. The road is unsurfaced and deteriorates as it gets further north, but it is possible to cycle all its length. It is open from May to September, and there are youth hostels, hotels and tourist stations along it. There are some side roads to the coast (few) and inland (very few). Summer is warm, with almost 24 hours of sunshine every day; the 'midnight sun' can be seen at Bodø between 1 June and 13 July and at North Cape between 12 May and 1 August. Every patch of soil is cultivated yet nearby are snow-covered peaks, gaunt rocks and glaciers.

A few cyclists each year reach this remote area but a lot of time, full equipment and stamina are necessary.

Climate
The climate in west Norway is similar to that of Britain. The Gulf Stream influence prevents great extremes of temperature and harbours as far north as Hammerfest are ice-free in winter. The summer is shorter but long hours of daylight help to raise summer temperatures. As in Britain, rain can fall anywhere at any time in summer; the Balestrand/Bergen/Stavanger coastal strip is often wet. In the eastern part of the country it is drier but the annual range of temperature is greater.

The best time for cycling in Norway is between late June and early September. In winter there is heavy snow on the mountains and it often reaches the lowlands. Roads are blocked by snow.

Language
English is widely spoken.

Maps
Cappelen 1:325,000 (three sheets cover the country).
Cappelen 1:400,000 (two sheets cover the country).

Poland

Getting there
Rail/sea   There is an evening departure daily from London (Liverpool Street) via Harwich/Hook of Holland–

Amersfoort–Osnabruck–Hannover–Berlin to Warsaw, and
a morning departure daily from London (Victoria) via
Dover/Ostend–Cologne–Berlin to Warsaw. There are
through coaches from the Hook of Holland to Warsaw
and from Ostend to Warsaw. Polish Ocean lines operate a
fortnightly passenger/cargo vessel between Tilbury and
Gdynia (three days' journey).

Air   Several flights are operated daily between London
(Heathrow) and Warsaw.

Travelling in Poland

There is a good railway network and a frequent service
of coaches between large towns. Bus fares are higher than
train fares, and buses do not convey cycles.

Cycling

A good road system covers most of the country. Surfaces
are generally good, and motor traffic light. All spares
should be taken.

Accommodation

There are about 300 youth hostels run by the
internationally-affiliated organisation, and at least as
many simpler hostels and huts run by the Polish Touring
Society (P.T.T.K.). Meals are provided at very
few. There are plenty of hotels of various grades, and of
restaurants and cafés.

Some touring areas

The North   The north is mostly lowlying, but is relieved
by hills and lakes left by glaciers to form attractive
scenery north and north-west of Warsaw. These areas are
readily accessible from the port of Gdynia. There are
many towns and villages which are picturesque and of
historic interest.

Central Poland   Poznan is the centre of a low-lying area in the west of the country, exploration of which can be combined with a tour of the middle and upper valleys of the Vistula, including Warsaw and the low hills stretching to the frontier with the U.S.S.R.

The South   Here the mountains rise along the entire frontier with Czechoslovakia. They include the High Tatra, south of Krakow, a spectacular region of crystalline rocks, Rysy being the highest summit in the country (8,200 ft., 2,500 m). It is all fine touring country, but the road system dictates a zig-zag ride across the grain of the hills rather than a straight journey along them. There are several National Parks in each of these areas.

Climate   Warm, moist Atlantic winds reach as far as Poland, where they alternate with cold, dry winds from the east. Rainfall is moderate and the temperature ranges from a winter average of freezing to warm summer months when inland afternoon averages are in the mid-seventies Fahrenheit (24°C.).

Language
Very little English is spoken.

Maps
For route planning: Kummerley & Frey 1:1,000,000 (one sheet covers the country).

   Other maps are not easily obtainable, but the P.P.W.K. (Warsaw) publishes useful regional tourist maps on various scales.

Portugal

Getting there
Rail/sea   Certain services from London (Victoria) to Paris connect with trains to Oporto and Lisbon, allowing time

to ride between Paris termini. Note that on journeys to Portugal, cycles should be registered from Paris (Gare d'Austerlitz) to their destination (unlike Spanish destinations, q.v.). A change of train at the Spanish frontier is usual due to the change of railway gauge.

Air   There are direct flights from London (Heathrow) to Lisbon and Faro.

Sea   There is a direct car ferry (cycles accepted) three times weekly between Southampton and Lisbon. The voyage takes 42 hours. Early booking is essential.

Travelling in Portugal
Railways extend along most of the coastline and there are a few inland branches. Trains are slow. There is an adequate bus system and cycles are transported. Photography should be limited to the usual tourist subjects, and care taken not to take any subjects of military or strategic interest.

Cycling
Most roads are well surfaced but some inland minor roads are not; some towns have cobbled streets. Cycles must be fitted with a bell.

Accommodation
There are few youth hostels in Portugal. There is plenty of other accommodation everywhere which is uniformly good and moderate in price. Hotels are carefully graded, and there are also *estalagem* (inns), *pousada (*state inns), *residencias* (boarding houses) and other overnight boarding houses. The official accommodation guides are particularly accurate and reliable.

Some touring areas
The North   The area north of the Tagus is hilly, and the centre and north-east mountainous, with a coastal plain.

Deep river valleys cut from east to west. The hill scenery is rugged, but elsewhere the landscape changes with the many uses to which the land is put. It is a fine part of the country for cycle touring, best reached from Oporto.

The South   South of the Tagus the landscape is equally diverse with areas of woodland (for cork and rubber) and wheatfields and tracts of heathland. The southernmost province, the Algarve, has arid sandy tracts and the coastline is almost North African in character where increasing popularity has led to the creation of many villa developments.

Climate
The climate is equable and Atlantic-influenced, with on-shore breezes tempering the summer heat which can occur on the coast. The western coasts and the mountain areas receive most rainfall, and heavy storms are some-times experienced in summer. Fogs are quite common on the Atlantic coast. The Algarve and the eastern strip of the country are often hot in summer.

Language
Very few people speak English.

Maps
Michelin sheet 37 1:500,000 (adequate for all purposes).
    There are no other up-to-date maps of the country.

Rumania

Getting there
Rail/sea   There is a daily service from London (Victoria) via Dover/Calais to Paris (change termini)–Stuttgart–

Salzburg–Vienna–Budapest–Bucharest, a change of train
being necessary in Vienna. The journey takes about 48
hours. There is also a daily service from Basel,
Switzerland (q.v.) via Innsbruck–Graz–Vienna–Budapest–
Bucharest, with through carriages all the way (35 hours).
Air   There is a daily direct flight from London
(Heathrow) to Bucharest. Other daily services involve a
change of aircraft at one of many continental airports.

Travelling in Rumania
The rail network is not extensive and much of it is single
track, but main lines radiate from Bucharest to the major
provincial towns (and on to adjacent countries). Inter-
provincial lines are virtually non-existent.

Cycling
Conditions are similar to those in Hungary, i.e. there is a
good network of generally quiet roads but their surfaces
vary in quality.

Accommodation
This is again similar to Hungary, with an adequate
number of hotels.

Some touring areas
The Western Plain   A small lowland area, this farming
district adjoins Hungary and Yugoslavia (into which
countries the plain extends). The chief town Timisoara
has an old town built round a fortress.
The Carpathian Mountains   This high range dominates
central Rumania, entering the country from the Soviet
Ukraine in the north and extending south and south-west
to enter Yugoslavia. The mountains are highest in the
south, with several peaks over 8,200 ft. (2,500 m). Many
large valleys and gorges form natural road routes and the

cyclist is able to make a comprehensive tour of the range.
There are extensive forests.

The South-East   Here is a broad semi-circular plain, with
Bucharest in the centre. Rice, tobacco and grapes are
among the crops cultivated and there is little other
industry. The large, marshy Danube delta separates the
semi-circle from the coastal plain on the Black Sea, where
Rumania has a coastline of 125 miles (200 km). Constanta
to the south is the main resort and port; to the north lies
the Dobrogea, where the coast has lagoons, spits and
cliffs and is difficult of access.

Climate
Winters are freezing and summers hot, the extremes being
somewhat greater in the east than in the west. In between,
the Carpathians have the coolest summers, and the highest
rainfall. June has the highest total rainfall of any month
in Rumania.

Language
Very little English is spoken anywhere.

Maps
Maps are virtually unobtainable; an atlas and guides
should be used.

Spain

Getting there
Rail/sea   Certain services from London (Victoria) to Paris
connect with trains to Barcelona and Madrid, allowing
time to ride between Paris termini. Note that on journeys
to Spain, cycles should be registered separately for the

three sections of the journey – London to Paris, Paris to
the Spanish frontier, and from the frontier to the final
destination – and that except for a few through sleeping
car services, a change of train is necessary at the Spanish
frontier due to the change of railway gauge. In the
summer season there are through trains from Boulogne to
the Spanish frontier station of Irun (for Madrid) and Port
Bou (for Barcelona).

Air   Direct flights operate from London to Madrid, and
other major cities such as Alicante, Barcelona, Gerona,
Malaga, San Sebastian and Seville, and to the island of
Majorca (Palma). There are connecting flights from
Belfast, Edinburgh, Glasgow and Manchester.

Sea   Ferries sail every four days in the summer season
from Southampton to Bilbao and Santander, and twice a
week from Southampton to San Sebastian. It is advisable
to book for these services five to six months in advance.

Travelling in Spain
There is a good rail system. Many trains are 'express' and
passengers are not permitted to board them unless they
hold a seat reservation or their tickets have been endorsed
with the train number and date at the starting station.
Supplements are payable on these trains. Stopping and
branch line trains are slow, and often crowded. It is
advisable to load the cycle on the train oneself. Bus
services vary in different parts of the country; cycles are
not conveyed. There is a good internal air service
between Madrid and the principal provincial towns, and
between provincial towns. Photography should be limited
to the usual tourist subjects, and care taken not to
include any subjects of military or strategic interest.

Cycling
Most main roads are well surfaced but many secondary

roads are rough. The latter are generally better in the north of the country and deteriorate as one goes south. Cycles must be fitted with a bell.

Accommodation
Youth hostels are widely spaced but there is reasonable coverage round the coast. Some provide only for males, and some only for females. There are hotels and *pensions* in towns and large villages; *fondas* (inns) are usually found in small towns, and *posadas* in villages, where simple but reasonably priced accommodation is provided.

Camping on public land is permitted and on private land with the owner's consent. It is not permitted (a) within 1 km of a town; (b) within 50 m of a main road; (c) within 150 m of waters supplying reservoirs; (d) in the vicinity of buildings of historic interest; (e) in shooting or fishing regions; (f) in forestry without the authority of the *Servicio Forestal*. Local authorities may prohibit camping elsewhere. Groups of more than ten campers, or more than three tents, must camp at authorised sites.

Some touring areas
The Pyrenees   A cycle tour in the Pyrenees involves crossing and recrossing between France and Spain several times, if they are to be fully explored. The difference in cultures on each side of the border is marked. Adequate minor roads with good surfaces exist along the length of the Pyrenees but some fine areas are accessible only by rough roads.
Central Spain   Around Madrid lies the *Meseta*. a large central plateau crossed by several *sierra* – long, jagged mountain ranges. There is much wild touring country, often sparsely populated. In this area, as in others in remote Spain, it is advisable to carry food supplies for a couple of days.

The South   150 miles (240 km) south of Madrid, the
Meseta ends abruptly, giving way to the narrow valley of
the Guadalquiver (Andalusia) with the heights of Granada
beyond – including the Sierra Nevada – before the
Mediterranean coast is reached.

The Coast   The highly-developed coast of the Costa Brava
in the north-east is unlikely to attract the cycle tourist
seeking quiet surroundings, but the rest of the extensive
Spanish coastline offers good touring with the opportunity
of side trips into the hinterlands. The Biscay coast – San
Sebastian, Santander, La Coruna – and the Mediterranean
coast – Valencia, Cartagena, Malaga – are especially good.

Climate

This varies greatly, like the landscapes of Spain. Frequent
rain and mist mar the northern coast even in summer.
Southern and central Spain experience great heat in
summer; the Mediterranean provinces are a little cooler
but very humid. Apart from in the north, rainfall is not
great though the central plateau is usually wet during
March and April.

Language

Very few people have a knowledge of English.

Maps

For route planning: Michelin sheet 990 1:1,000,000
(indicates types of road surface).

    For detailed route finding: Michelin 1:400,000 (two
sheets cover the country).

Notes

Informal holiday wear is increasingly acceptable in
popular resorts, but care should be taken not to offend.
Shorts may be worn for cycling, but trousers should be

handy for wear when walking in public places, when
shopping and when seeking accommodation. Ladies
should wear trousers or a skirt.

   Gibraltar is not at present accessible from Spain (only
by sea).

Sweden

Getting there
Rail/sea   The best route from England is from London
(Liverpool Street) to Tilbury, then the Swedish Lloyd
boat to Gothenburg; sailings are four or five times a week
in summer and three times a week at other times. There is
a thrice-weekly service from Immingham to Gothenburg
operated by Tor Line. All these services are heavily used
and it is advisable to make bookings six months in
advance.

   The services to Copenhagen (see Denmark section) also
have connections to Sweden via the Copenhagen/
Halsingborg ferry.

   From both Gothenburg and Halsingborg there are rail
connections to Malmö, Stockholm and the north.
Air   There are frequent flights from London (Heathrow)
to Stockholm.

Travelling in Sweden
There is an extensive railway system in the south, and a
line from Stockholm to Boden and Abisko in the north
with a branch to Storlien (and on to Trondheim, Norway).
The service is of a high standard, and trains and stations
well appointed. Holiday tickets are available which show
an appreciable reduction in fare if good use is made of the
railway.

There are also very many coach and bus services;
cycles are carried on long-distance buses.

Cycling
The trunk roads in the south carry a good deal of traffic.
These, and other main roads everywhere (though there
are few in the north) have good surfaces. Secondary roads
are generally unsurfaced and have dust or loose gravel
with some potholes. It is necessary on these roads to
remove the dust from the chain and gear mechanism from
time to time.

All spares should be taken, though most towns have a
cycle shop where running repairs are undertaken.

Sweden is not as hilly as might be expected, apart from
the north-west corner.

Accommodation
There are many youth hostels but the majority are small
and seasonal. They are of a good standard. In the
highlands, the Swedish Touring Club maintains various
grades of mountain lodges and huts; membership of the
club is a prerequisite of their use. Guest houses and
hotels are plentiful in the south but less so as one travels
north.

Most towns have a number of restaurants according to
their size, the *konsum* or *mjolkbar* offering good food at
reasonable prices. Even small villages have a *konditori*
where coffee and pastries are obtainable.

Except where specifically forbidden by notice, camping
is allowed on public and private land but permission
should be sought.

Some touring areas
Sweden extends for almost 1,000 miles (1,600 km) from
north to south and is bordered by the sea on three sides.

The coastline is impressive, with many indentations, but lacks fjords of Norwegian grandeur.

The South   Between Halmstad and Malmö is a fertile plain reminiscent of Denmark; the buildings too have a Danish aspect resulting from a long period of Danish rule. The area from Malmö to Kalmar is more rugged with pleasant and historic towns inland and on the coast, some of the latter being popular resorts.

North-east of Gothenburg lie the great lakes Vanern and Vattern. There are many viewpoints from the lakeside roads, waterfalls, forests and ancient towns.

Central Sweden   From Stockholm to Orebro and back round Lake Malaren makes a good 250-mile (400 km) tour. There is fine scenery, many castles and country houses, and the lake is dotted with many extremely beautiful islands. Uppsala, a university town with a cathedral and much else of interest, is reached by a short side trip from Sigtuna.

Further inland, Dalarna is perhaps the most picturesque region in Sweden, with lakes, dales and villages of great beauty.

The North   Sundsvall is a good starting point for a tour of Jamtland, where the mountainous area begins – there are 5,000 ft. (1,525 m) peaks near the Norwegian frontier. Valleys, forests and lakes (the road round Lake Storsjon is one of the most beautiful in the country) make for a varied charm difficult to surpass.

The far north is a wild and fascinating region of mountain masses, lakes and little vegetation. The more fertile coastal lowlands and the area near the Finnish frontier have a limited road system, but inland communications are by path and track in a region reserved for only the most intrepid cyclist – the real explorer.

Climate
The Swedish climate is dry, nowhere in the country
receiving more than 50″ (127 cm) of rain a year. Summer
is short: June, July and August in the south, and even
shorter in the north, but during these months the
sunlight is intense. Summer rain falls heavily but briefly.
The days are long in summer and very short in winter.

The south-west tends to be damper and mistier than
elsewhere.

Language
Most Swedes have a good knowledge of English, of the
other Scandinavian languages, and of German, with
which spoken Swedish has a clear affinity.

Maps
For all purposes: G.L.A. maps 1:1,000,000 (two sheets
cover the country).

Larger scale maps of Sweden are difficult to obtain, but
these sheets show all roads which are useful to the cyclist
though they lack topographical detail, which should be
taken from guide books and pamphlets.

Switzerland

Getting there
Rail/Sea   From the French channel ports of Calais and
Boulogne through trains run to Basel. There are
connecting services from London. More frequent trains
go from Paris to Basel. Some trains run beyond Basel to
other parts of Switzerland; there are frequent electric
trains from Basel to all parts of the country. For some

destinations in southern Switzerland, it may be more
convenient to travel via Paris and Vallorbe. Tickets may
be purchased in the U.K. for travel outward by one route
and back by another, at extra cost.

If rail travel in Switzerland is to exceed about 300 km
it will be worthwhile to buy a 'Swiss Holiday Ticket'.
There is a flat rate charge for this ticket but with it travel
between the Swiss frontier and the destination in
Switzerland (and vice versa) is charged at half fare. The
ticket further entitles the holder to up to five more rail
journeys at reduced rates, which shows a considerable
saving on some of the expensive mountain railways. The
ticket can also be issued in conjunction with air tickets to
Basel and Geneva.

Air   There are frequent services from London (Heathrow
and Gatwick) to Basel, Zurich and Geneva, and from
Birmingham and Manchester to Zurich.

Travelling in Switzerland
An excellent network of punctual and efficient railways
covers the country. Steamer services operate on the lakes
and in most cases rail tickets are interchangeable with
steamer tickets for all or part of journeys where there is a
choice between boat and train.
Postal coaches convey passengers and most of them take
cycles. They do not duplicate rail routes but start from
railway termini to reach places inaccessible by rail.

Cycling
Cycles must carry a bell. On mountain passes, precedence
must be given to postal coaches. Trams and trolleybuses
have priority at all times.

Cycles may be hired from all stations of the Swiss
Federal Railways and from stations on some private
railways. Two or three days' notice may have to be given

as in some cases the machines are sent from a central depot. They are unsuitable for anything more than local sightseeing rides. The cost varies according to the length of time the cycle is out, and there is a small extra charge if it is returned to a station other than the one from which it was hired.

Road surfaces in general are very good. In a few localities, notably Canton Zug, cobbled roads occur. The lesser-known Alpine passes are often unsurfaced for several miles on either side of the summits, and in winter frost and snow often damage the surfaces over the high passes like the St. Gotthard and St. Bernard.

Accommodation
There is a good network of well-appointed hostels. They are restricted to persons under 25 years of age except for leaders of parties. Other accommodation is plentiful, with many inns (*Gasthof, Gasthaus*) and small hotels. Many private houses offer *Zimmer* (see explanation under 'Accommodation in Germany'). Cafés and restaurants are also numerous.

Tourist information offices (*Verkehrsamt*) exist in most towns and at principal railway stations. They will assist in finding accommodation.

Some touring areas
The central lake district of the country offers pleasant touring – not too hilly, with splendid scenery and many historical associations and architectural features. This is the Bern–Thun–Interlaken–Lucern–Altdorf area where cycling can be alternated with steamer trips to make an enjoyable tour.
Ticino   South of the Gotthard range, this canton contains contrasting landscapes, rocky hills rising from fertile valleys and forests. The people are Italian-speaking and

churches and houses are Italian in style.

The Grisons   This is the largest and least populated
canton, much of it barren rock and ice upland where even
the valleys are often 5,000 ft. (1,525 m) above sea level.
In the valleys of the upper Rhine and of the Inn the
Romansch language is spoken – the only area where it
survives. Most people there also speak the official
language, German. There are many pretty valleys, and
some high passes; old castles and churches; and
spectacular feats of railway engineering enabling some of
the high roads to be attained the easy way if desired.

The Engadine   The 60-mile valley of the river Inn runs
from Maloja to the Austrian frontier in eastern
Switzerland. It is an area of low rainfall, strong sunshine
and cool nights where trees grow at 7,000 ft. (2,135 m)
above sea level or some 1,000 ft. (305 m) higher up than
in the rest of the country. Whitewashed stone houses,
often with painted decorations, have small windows with
iron grilles. Here the Alpine flowers abound in early
summer.

The Bernese Oberland   This lies on the northern slopes of
the Bernese Alps and is deservedly a very popular
holiday district. The impressive grandeur of the
mountains, the villages of chalets with wide overhanging
eaves and the many waterfalls and glaciers attract large
numbers of visitors and have led to the creation of a
highly-organised tourist industry even by Swiss
standards.

The Valais   The area around the hot and dusty (in
summer) valley of the upper Rhone through which a busy
road runs alongside river and railway, this is a canton in
which many old customs and traditions survive, including
in some places the distinctive costume for women on
Sundays. Although the main road is less than ideal for
cycling, it gives access to many worthwhile side roads

which lead to places of interest through fine countryside,
Aosta (over the Great St. Bernard pass), Chamonix, the
Val de Bagnes, Arolla, Zinal, Zermatt and Saas Fee among
them.

Climate
The range of climate in Switzerland is very great, being
influenced by numerous local features – height,
configuration of mountains and wind systems. The Fohn
is a warm south wind which occurs in the central
mountain area and raises the temperature considerably. It
blows most frequently in spring and autumn but can
occur at any time. The Bise is a cold north winter wind
affecting the 'Foreland', the plain between the Jura
mountains (French/Swiss border between the Rhone and
the Rhine) and the Alps. The Valais and the Engadine are
the driest regions; low southern slopes have mild, sunny
winters. Snow lies permanently above 9,000 ft. (2,745 m).

Language
French, German and Italian are spoken in Switzerland, an
approximate division being French in the west, German in
the centre and north, and Italian in the south. Many
people speak more than one of these languages. Quite a
lot of Swiss people throughout the country have a
knowledge of English.

Maps
For route planning. Kummerly & Fry sheet 1025
Switzerland 1:400,000 (coloured relief).
   For detailed route finding: Michelin 1:200,000 (four
sheets cover the country).

Liechtenstein

This small principality is situated between Austria and
Switzerland. It has an area of 62 square miles (16,055
hectares). The capital is Vaduz, and the area is
mountainous, the chief occupation being farming.
German is spoken and Swiss currency used.

Turkey-in-Europe

Getting there
Rail/sea   There is a daily service from London
(Victoria) via Dover/Calais – Paris (change termini)–
Milan–Trieste–Belgrade–Istanbul, with through carriages
from Paris to Istanbul. Departure from London is in the
early afternoon, and Istanbul is reached on the morning
of the fourth day. Alternative routes are London
(Victoria) via Dover/Ostend–Cologne–Munich–Salzburg–
Zagreb–Istanbul, and London (Liverpool Street) via
Harwich/Hook of Holland–Cologne, then the same route
to Istanbul. Journey times are similar to the above and on
both routes a change of train is necessary in Munich.

   Seat or sleeper reservations are compulsory from
Munich onwards.
Air   Direct flights leave daily from London (Heathrow) to
Istanbul.

Travelling in Turkey
The only railway line is the main line from Bulgaria (the
trunk link with the rest of Europe) but there is a branch
line into Greece. There is an adequate service of buses but
timetables should be ascertained in advance.

Cycling
There are two trunk roads, one entering Turkey at

Edirne from Bulgaria and the other entering the country
at Ipsala from Greece. They merge at Silviri for Istanbul.
These roads, and the Havsa–Kesan road between them in
the west, are broad smooth highways carrying fairly
heavy fast-moving traffic. Other roads are much less busy
and usually have reasonable surfaces.

Accommodation
The only youth hostel is in Istanbul; it is not affiliated to
the international federation. There are student hostels in a
few other large towns, which also have enquiry bureaux
where details of hotel, *pension* and camping possibilities
are obtainable. Accommodation is not easy to find in
summer. There are plenty of well-stocked shops for
provisions in all towns.

Touring
The cyclist entering Turkey by road should allow for a
delay of two hours at the frontier for customs formalities.
There are forms to be completed, one of which requires
much personal detail (including the date and place of
birth of parents, mother's maiden name, etc.) and full
details of the cycle are entered in one's passport and
cancelled when one leaves the country (this ensures that
the same machine is taken out as was brought in, and not
exchanged or sold in Turkey). For those entering by rail,
these formalities will take place at the arrival station.

   When leaving Turkey by road, there will also be a
delay at the frontier while exit formalities are gone
through. Registration of the cycle for despatch by rail
from Turkey to another country is not recommended; the
procedure can take a day to complete and even then the
machine may be heavily delayed en route, arriving at the
destination perhaps weeks, or even months, later.

   Only a very small part of Turkey is in Europe, and it is

quite unlike the rest of the country which lies across the Bosporus, in Asia. There are mosques, of course, and other signs of the orient, but the general way of life is European. The central and southern parts of the peninsula forming Turkey-in-Europe are surprisingly open and green, with large areas farmed and views over a wide, fertile landscape. Behind the Black Sea coast in the north there is a small area of pleasant hill country, and there is a similar area, smaller still, in the south overlooking the Sea of Marmara. Both of these coasts are relatively undeveloped. All of this part of Turkey could be covered in an interesting two-week tour.

Climate
It is quite cold between December and March, but summers are hot. Rainfall is moderate, but very heavy showers and storms (usually of short duration) can occur at any time. High winds occur all the year round, even in summer when the temperature is high, and they reduce (or increase!) cycling speed considerably.

Language
Few people speak English, though you will usually find someone in Istanbul who does.

Maps
Large-scale maps are difficult to obtain both in this country and in Turkey. Diligent enquiry may locate some 1:500,000 sheets, but it may be necessary to resort to road diagrams, produced for motorists, and to an atlas. These give little or no detail of the country, but suffice for this comparatively small area when used in conjunction with guide books and leaflets.

United Kingdom – England

Travelling in England
Main line railways radiate from London to all parts of the
country except the northern coast of the south-western
peninsula (Somerset, Devon and Cornwall) and the central
northern part of the country, though nowhere is more
than 30 miles or so from a railway. There are adequate
inter-provincial railways, but only a small number of
branch lines survive. Services are fast and frequent
between major centres, but less so on secondary routes.
Sunday services are less frequent and slower than
weekday ones. Local and long-distance bus and coach
services cover the country. Cycles are not conveyed on
these.

Internal air services operate frequently between the
major cities of the United Kingdom.

Cycling
The majority of 'A' roads carry heavy traffic, but the
cycle tourist is at no disadvantage as there is a complex
network of 'B' and unclassified roads which reach every
town, village and hamlet in the country; many of these
roads are used only by residential and service traffic.

There are few cycle paths, and except in the case of a
few very short lengths alongside particularly busy roads,
their use is not obligatory. Where it is, it is indicated by
the international circular blue sign with the white outline
of a cycle in the centre.

In country areas some good cycling is to be had on
'bridleways' (unsurfaced but rideable tracks) which
cyclists may legally use.

For night riding, a white front lamp and a red rear
lamp conforming to official specification must be used.
A red rear reflector is also compulsory but it may be

combined with the rear lamp.

All towns have a cycle shop but not all of them stock a wide range of parts. Repairs cannot usually be undertaken quickly.

Accommodation

There is a large number of youth hostels situated in the more popular touring areas and in large towns, with intermediate hostels strategically located to connect. There are as many hotels in inland towns as their size and importance warrant, and coastal resorts are well provided with them. Private houses and small *pension*-type establishments are numerous in all but the largest industrial centres, and farmhouses offering accommodation are common in the countryside. The Cyclists' Touring Club publishes an annual handbook for its members which lists recommended addresses at which to stay when touring.

Casual accommodation is often difficult to find at peak holiday times – Easter, the last weekend in May, mid-July to early September, and at Christmas. At these periods advance reservation is advised.

There are many municipal camping sites round the coast of England and some inland. In National Parks camping is closely controlled, as it is also in state forests, where it is sometimes not allowed. The Camping Club of Great Britain and Ireland has a large number of listed sites for its members. Permission to camp on private land is rarely refused to the occasional cycle-camper or small group. (This applies to private land within National Parks and elsewhere.)

Some touring areas

England is unique in having so much diverse scenery and

so many varied characteristics within such a small country. Every part of it is of interest; and this applies even to the major cities and industrial centres. Some of the outstanding areas of the countryside are mentioned below; several are easily combined in a single cycle tour of two or three weeks. Historic buildings and sites abound, as do styles of domestic local architecture.

The South-East   Despite the domination of London there is much attractive countryside; south of London between the two ranges of low chalk hills (the North and South Downs) there is a wealth of farmland, orchards, woods and quiet villages. North-west of London are the chalk Chiltern Hills, and north and north-east lie quiet villages in a flatter countryside.

The South-West   West of the cathedral cities of Salisbury and Winchester are the New Forest, the pastoral downland of Dorset, the uplands of Somerset and Devon (Blackdown, Brendon and Quantock hills, Exmoor, Dartmoor) and the rugged county of Cornwall forming the end of the peninsula. The coastline is particularly varied and interesting for all its length.

The Cotswolds and Shakespeare Country   The limestone Cotswold hills of Gloucestershire and Oxfordshire are a very popular cycle touring area where the stone is used for buildings and for walls instead of hedges and fences. The result is a mellow individuality about the countryside and a dignity about the small towns and villages. Immediately to the north are lowlands with timber and thatch villages and historic towns, including Stratford-on-Avon, the birthplace of Shakespeare. Its attraction is marred by crowds of tourists and the manner in which they are catered for.

The Midlands   The Coventry/Birmingham/Wolverhampton conurbations are centres of heavy industry, as are Stafford, Derby, Nottingham, Leicester and Rugby. They

nevertheless contain much of interest, and they are separated by tracts of open country of surprising richness so close to areas of high development.

East Anglia   The eastern counties of Suffolk and Norfolk with parts of neighbouring counties form the quietest and driest corner of England. Generally flat, it is an area of unhurried charm, of farmlands and picturesque villages and towns. Norwich, the largest city, is a noble one.

The Welsh Border   Between Chepstow and Chester lie the Wye Valley and the Forest of Dean, the hill country of Herefordshire and Shropshire and a series of historic towns including Hereford, Ludlow and Shrewsbury. It is hilly country, with abbeys, castles and 'black and white' timbered houses.

The Peak District   This is not a district with peaks, but a distinctive upland dark sandstone area surrounding a limestone core where there is much good hill country of wild character.

The Yorkshire Dales   The rivers flowing through west Yorkshire from the Pennine hills form valleys of individual beauty. These sweeping 'dales' have waterfalls, bare fellsides, stone villages, great houses and historic ruins in profusion.

The Lake District   This compact district of the north-west has all the character of a mountain region in miniature: hills – several summits are over 3,000 ft. (915 m) including the highest in England, Scafell, which is 3,210 ft (979 m), valleys and lakes in startling succession give the impression of much greater proportions. Roads reach 1,500 ft. (457 m), often climbing very steeply for a mile or two.

The North-East   Northumberland and Durham are less

Cyclists enjoying a New Year's Day run in Surrey

visited by touring cyclists than their attractions merit.
The county of Northumberland is one of the most thinly
populated in England and roads, with the exception of
the Darlington/Newcastle/Scotland main route, are very
quiet. It is bold, moorland country, with wide views,
large forests, and many special points of interest such as
the Roman Wall, Alnwick Castle, Coquet Dale and
Durham cathedral.

Climate
The English climate is very variable and unpredictable.
South-west winds from the Atlantic prevail, making it
generally mild and humid and resulting in high rainfall in
the west (especially the hill districts). Rainfall in the east
is much lower. Western districts often have 60″ (152 cm)
of rain annually whilst in the east half this amount is
normal. Temperature decreases from south to north in
summer and from west to east in winter. Extremes are
rare but in summer winds from eastern Europe or the
Mediterranean sometimes bring hot spells, and in winter
an east or north-east wind can bring a freezing spell.

Language
Regional dialects of the language persist in most areas and
some, e.g. the Tyneside accent, are not easy to
understand.

Maps
For route planning: Ordnance Survey 1:625,000 (two
sheets cover the country) and Bartholomews 1:1,000,000
(one sheet).

For detailed route finding: Bartholomews 1:100,000
(approximately 40 sheets cover the country) and
Ordnance Survey 1:50,000 (see page 63. About 110 of
these sheets cover the country. They are needed only

for areas where specially comprehensive detail is
required. Very useful tourist sheets are published to this
scale for a number of areas of special attraction.)

United Kingdom – Scotland

Travelling in Scotland
Main lines from London with very fast trains run to
Glasgow via Carlisle and to Edinburgh via Newcastle.
There is a line from Carlisle to Edinburgh and one from
Carlisle to Dumfries, Kilmarnock and Glasgow. There are
main lines northward to Perth, Dundee, Aberdeen and
Inverness, and subsidiary lines serve some of the south-
west and north-east coasts. Bus services in the populous
areas are good, but in the remote areas one bus a day –
except on Sundays – is the rule. Cycles are not carried.

  There are steamer services to the Western Isles and the
Orkneys and Shetlands for which the timings should be
ascertained as required. There is no service on Sundays.

Cycling
Main roads in the south are busy but there are many
by-roads for the cyclist. All are well surfaced. The north
is served by few roads and even the 'A' routes are often
narrow lanes on which cars have difficulty in passing; in
the summer these roads can get congested with
holidaymakers and the cycle tourist needs to plan route
and riding times with care to avoid the traffic as much as
possible. All necessary spares should be carried. There
are few cycle shops outside Glasgow and Edinburgh and
supplies are limited at those.

Accommodation
There is good coverage of youth hostels. Other

accommodation of all kinds is plentiful in the south and
central areas, but less so in the north which is thinly
settled. Most hamlets have houses where bed and
breakfast are provided, but the solo traveller is
sometimes not welcomed. Places of any size have a tourist
information bureau in summer open until 7 or 8 p.m.
where advice on accommodation is available. In the north,
it is advisable to carry a food supply as shops and cafés
are often few and far between.

Some touring areas
The South-West   This lesser-known area has quiet,
rolling countryside and a fine coastline varying from
rocky headlands to long sandy beaches. There are holiday
resorts on the south bank of the Clyde, and the islands of

*Near the Scottish border there is plenty of open country with quiet
roads*

Arran and Bute are within easy reach.

Loch Lomond and Central Highlands   Loch Lomond is large, set in magnificent mountain scenery, and close to the small Trossach range. To the north are the Central Highlands, the most easily accessible part of the Highlands. Loch Earn and Loch Tay lie in the shadows of high peaks, and streams rush down gorges and glens to join them.

The Northern Highlands   West and north of the 'Great Glen' (Fort William–Inverness) is the finest scenery in Scotland. It is a wild area, much of it barren and exposed. Sea lochs indent the coast, some reminiscent of the fjords of Norway.

The Islands   All but the very small islands have surfaced roads enabling the cycle tourist to explore them; the more intrepid can use rough tracks to do so more extensively.

Climate

The climate differs between east and west; the former is colder, often with heavy snow in winter, but is drier in summer. Rainfall is high in the north-west – up to 150″ (380 cm) annually – but decreases greatly towards the south. High winds are common. June is often the best month with September and October often providing fine spells too, but the weather can change hourly (and frequently does).

Language

Gaelic is still spoken by many people in the north-west but they all speak English also.

Maps

For tour planning: Ordnance Survey 1:625,000 (one sheet) and Bartholomews 1:1,000,000 (one sheet).

For detailed route planning: Bartholomews 1:100,000 (approximately 25 sheets cover the country) and Ordnance Survey 1:50,000 (approximately 75 sheets cover the country. These are needed only for areas where specially comprehensive detail is required. Very useful tourist sheets are published to this scale for a few areas of special attraction).

United Kingdom – Wales

Travelling in Wales
Main railway lines run from Chester along the north coast to Holyhead (Isle of Anglesey) and from Bristol along the south coast to Fishguard, both with through fast trains from London. The only other lines are branches from Shrewsbury through central Wales to the coast between Aberystwyth and Pwllheli and from Shrewsbury south-west to Llanelli and Newport (Gwent), both junctions with the south coast line. There are good local bus services in coastal areas but the interior is sparsely served and long-distance routes are few. Cycles are not conveyed. Tourist attractions include several narrow-gauge railways in scenic districts.

Cycling
Main roads in the south-east of the country, and the road along the northern coast, carry heavy traffic, as does the west coast road during the holiday season. The roads in the interior are mostly narrow and winding and although they occasionally get congested locally with holiday traffic, conditions are normally very good for cycle touring. All roads have good surfaces. Wales is well known for the number of 'rough-stuff' hill crossings

which may be made by cycle over unsurfaced tracks and paths, not all of them rideable.

Accommodation
The youth hostels are well sited in most areas, and are between 15 and 30 miles apart. Note that in some districts public houses do not open on Sundays.

Some touring areas
The North   The northern end of the Cambrian mountains form the Snowdonia district. Snowdon is the highest mountain in Wales at 3,560 ft. (1,086 m). The scree or forest covered hills, valleys with waterfalls and upland farms form a rugged landscape. The Isle of Anglesey and the Lleyn peninsula are flatter, more pastoral, with pleasant inland and coastal fishing villages.
Mid-Wales   The coast has numerous small resorts and several fine estuaries but the interior is thinly populated and often wild. The man-made lakes (reservoirs) are somewhat out of character but add variety to the scene, which is one of rolling hills, forestry patchwork, wooded valleys and farms.
South Wales   The south-west has a splendid coastline especially between Cardigan and Pembroke, and attractive undulating country inland which extends throughout the county of Dyfed, a particular favourite for British cyclists because of its quiet nature and tidy villages as well as the network of minor roads and tracks over and between the hills.

The southern part of the county of Powys includes the Brecon Beacons, impressive mountains, and nearby are the brooding Black mountains.

Only a narrow strip of the country between Llanelli and Newport, and much of the small county of mid-Glamorgan, are given over to industry and mining.

Climate
It is generally wetter than in England, but the climate is otherwise similar.

Language
Welsh is spoken by a million people in Wales (about a third of the population) and is in common use in many areas. Very few, however, do not speak English and there is no language problem.

Maps
For route planning: Ordnance Survey 1:625,000 (one sheet) and Bartholomews 1:1,000,000 (one sheet).

For detailed route finding: Bartholomews 1:100,000 (eight sheets cover the country) and Ordnance Survey 1:50,000 (needed only for areas where specially comprehensive detail is required).

United Kingdom – Northern Ireland

Getting there
Rail/sea   There is a nightly service (except on Saturdays) from Stranraer (Scotland) to Larne, with rail connections from London, Glasgow and provincial centres. Nightly services (except on Sundays) run between Liverpool and Belfast, and Glasgow and Belfast. Rail connections are by ordinary services. In summer a daytime sailing operates daily between Ardrossan (Scotland) and Belfast.
Air   There are frequent services between the following cities and Belfast: London, Birmingham, Leeds, Manchester, Newcastle-upon-Tyne, Edinburgh and Glasgow.

From the Irish Republic   There are rail and air services between Dublin and Belfast. The cyclist can ride across any border road. There is a customs examination for travellers between the Republic and Northern Ireland and vice versa.

Travelling in Northern Ireland
The main railway line is from the border with the Republic to Belfast, thence to Londonderry with a branch to Larne. Other branches are very few. There is a good bus system and cycles are sometimes conveyed. British money is used (and unofficially that of the Republic is too).

Cycling
All roads have very good surfaces and apart from the Belfast/Londonderry main road they carry little traffic. All spares needed should be carried. Regulations are the same as in England.

Accommodation
Youth hostels are mostly on the Antrim coast and in the Mourne Mountains. Restaurants and cafés are few except in Belfast but meals can be obtained in most towns at hotels or perhaps a restaurant. Hotel and boarding house accommodation is adequate. Camping is not advised.

Some touring areas
The Antrim Coast   From Larne to Londonderry runs the Antrim coast road, with the sea below on one side and moorland and glens on the other. Fine scenery and fishing villages, seaside resorts and the Giant's Causeway (a columnar formation of lava of great extent) make excellent touring.

The Mourne Mountains   This compact but beautiful range
lies between Newry and Belfast, with good valleys and
views, and fishing villages on the coast as well as the
holiday resort of Newcastle.
The Sperrin Mountains   These lie inland between
Londonderry and Belfast and in addition to offering good
cycling in pleasant and interesting countryside the area
allows one to meet the real countryman.

Climate
The climate is similar to that of the Republic.

Maps
For all purposes: Bartholomew $\frac{1}{4}'' = 1$ mile (1:250,000)
(one sheet covers all but a very small part of the country).

Yugoslavia

Getting there
Note that the British Visitors' Passport is not acceptable in
Yugoslavia and a full passport must be held.
Accompanied cycles to Yugoslavia must be registered
through to their destination in that country. They must
be checked at the Austrian and Yugoslav frontiers for
Customs clearance, or they may be taken off the train.
(This check is not necessary at the Belgian and German
frontiers.) Cyclists returning from country stations in
Yugoslavia should register their cycles to Belgrade or
Zagreb (according to route) and then register them again
to Britain, otherwise they will certainly suffer delay,
which could be prolonged.
Rail/sea   The route is via Dover/Ostend to Salzburg. The
Tauern Express goes daily all the year round to Jesenice,

Ljubljana, Zagreb, Belgrade, Skopje. The Dalmatian
Express, a daily service in summer only, goes to Rijeka
via Ljubljana. The Yugoslavia Express, a nightly service
during the peak holiday season only, goes to Rijeka via
Ljubljana. Journey times are: to Ljubljana, 28 hours; to
Zagreb, 30 hours; to Belgrade, 37 hours; to Rijeka, 31
hours.
Air   Regular flights go from London (Heathrow) to
Dubrovnik and Zagreb; also to Venice, a handy
jumping-off point for Yugoslavia.

Travelling in Yugoslavia
There is an adequate rail network but speeds are slow;
trains average about 20 m.p.h. and are infrequent. Local
buses and coaches cover the more remote places but
cycles are not conveyed. The resorts and islands of the
Dalmatian coast are connected by steamers. Express boats
link them at major places with Venice, Trieste or Piraeus.

   Tourists in remote parts of the country should carry
food supplies for a couple of days and some form of
cooking equipment. There are some appreciable distances
without much in the way of shops, and the shops in some
small villages run out of supplies of perishable foods early
in the day as they are accustomed to catering only for a
small, regular demand. They do not always have supplies
of tinned food, and convenience foods are rare.

   In view of the poor roads in such parts it is unwise to
plan to cover more than 30–40 miles a day.

   Do not loiter in the vicinity of, or photograph, military
establishments or strategic installations.

Cycling
The Adriatic coast road has a tarmac surface for the
whole of its length, and most other roads in the north and
west of the country have good surfaces. Some, however,

and most of the minor roads, are in bad condition. In the eastern part of Yugoslavia a good road surface is the exception rather than the rule.

Cycling is not permitted in some main thoroughfares in major towns. In the Ljubljana–Zagreb area certain major roads have been designated motorways and cycling is not permitted on them; this also applies to some roads south of Belgrade. The necessary detours are lengthy and over rough roads but are invariably worthwhile. A road map is published annually showing the current state of road surfaces in the country – gravel surfaces are called 'macadam' – and is obtainable from the Yugoslav Tourist Office. All cyclists intending to visit the country should obtain a copy.

Accommodation

The Dalmatian coast is well supplied with hotels and guest houses but elsewhere there is a scarcity of accommodation. All tourists are required to stay at officially appointed addresses, and in tourist resorts letting is arranged by the tourist office (*Putnik* office) to whom payment is made.

Camping also is officially allowed only on authorised sites, of which there are plenty in the western part of the country.

In the centre, east and south of Yugoslavia, however, hotels and camping sites are few and far between. Private homes will often arrange accommodation, and good camp sites can be found in these areas, but the search for either should be made in good time each day.

There are some 30 youth hostels. They are very crowded in summer, especially as there is no limit to the length of stay and they are booked up by commercial travel agents. No hostels in Yugoslavia provide cooking facilities.

Good restaurants are found only in the coastal resorts and larger inland centres. Meals are substantial but service is very slow; an hour or more usually elapses between placing an order and receiving the food. Hungry cyclists should order a meal as soon as they arrive at their hotel or restaurant to be sure of getting it before they collapse. The interval can be used to do a bit of sightseeing or shopping.

Some touring areas
The six parts of Yugoslavia are here called 'provinces' for clarity but they are in fact autonomous republics within the Federal Republic of Yugoslavia.

Slovenia and Croatia   These two northernmost provinces provide a good tour in their own right or can be made the object of a short visit during a tour in south-eastern Austria. Ljubljana is reached by rail or by cycle over the Würzen pass (3,400 ft. or 1,037 m), the latter giving the opportunity to visit Lake Bled and its fascinating surroundings. A tour via Maribor, Zagreb, Plitvicka, Obrovac and Rijeka and back to Ljubljana through Koper takes in mountain scenery, gorges, the Plitvice National Park with many lakes at different levels and a good stretch of the Adriatic coast.

Bosnia–Herzegovina   In this central province where east meets west; the contrast between developments in the Austro–Hungarian period and those of the Turkish period is marked. The area contains the popular and historic resorts of Dubrovnik and Mostar, Sarajevo and Jajce.

Serbia   Here are the cities of Belgrade and Nis, with much industry which is also developing in the line of country between them. Elsewhere there is much thinly-populated farmland, pleasant valleys and rolling hills.

Macedonia and Montenegro   This mountainous and rugged district, with towns ancient and modern, is rich in

sites and monuments of Greek, Roman and religious
interest.

Climate
Most of the country is very hot in July and August (the
Julian Alps and the north of the country are a little
cooler than the rest) and rainfall is minimal. The coastal
strip enjoys a mild winter but further inland the winters
are cold.

Language
English is understood by a limited number of people in a
few well-known resorts only. A knowledge of German is
useful in most parts of Yugoslavia but make it known
that you are not German if speaking that language.

A section of the crowd attending a cycle touring rally in Surrey

Maps
For route planning: Kummerley & Frey 1:1,000,000.
For detailed route finding: Freytag & Berndt 1:600,000
(two sheets cover the country).
Larger scale maps are not available in the U.K.

Note
Cycle touring is not at present possible in the U.S.S.R. No
tourists are permitted to enter Albania, the small
republic on the Adriatic between Yugoslavia and Greece.

11

What it's really like

Cycle-Camping in Scotland

They do say that June and September are the best times for visiting Scotland, and it is true that the weather there during those months is often better than in July and August. So I decided to go in June, which has the added advantage that the hours of daylight are then at their longest. The roads and tourist areas are less busy than in high summer, too.

For a long time I had wanted to explore the far north-west by cycle, and at last the opportunity to do so came along. I knew it to be a region much favoured by cycle tourists, but as far as I was concerned it was an unknown country, reputed to be unlike any other part of Britain; the map certainly seemed to indicate a wild and thinly populated place – the sort where camping would be good, and where complete self-sufficiency might be wise in view of the long distances without habitation.

My sense of pleasant anticipation as I packed my camping kit and other gear in my saddle bag and panniers was every bit as keen as when preparing for a tour much further afield. Not much experience is needed to learn that the weather in these islands is not always related to the calendar, so plenty of warm clothing and wet-weather wear was included. The all-up weight of bicycle and bags approached 60 lb. (27·2 kg) which is about as low as can be managed when you are carrying sufficient to be prepared for anything.

The tour started at Glasgow, reached by train. It doesn't take a cyclist long to get clear of even such a large city as Glasgow, and I and two other cyclists who had by chance travelled on the same train were soon through the suburbs. Mark and Jack pedalled off for the Fintry Hills and beyond, and I was soon wheeling along the shores of Loch Lomond, and looking for a site to pitch my tent.

The hills fell so steeply to the loch that there wasn't room to pitch even my small tent, and as I did not want to travel far in what was left of the day after the long train journey, I turned at Tarbet to the head of Loch Long at Arrochar, where a site was quickly found.

The first night out, whatever sort of accommodation I am using, is always the occasion of repacking my bags. For a journey with the cycle, all is packed with an eye to security and ease of handling, rather than with accessibility on the road in mind. Once on the road, it is more important to have items packed in accessibility relative to frequency of need. Security is not forgotten, but the camera, for example, can be carried conveniently in a cycle bag when cycling – on the train, valuable items are carried on one's person.

Then there is camp routine. Pitching a small, light-weight tent is simplicity itself, even in the rain or the dark. (How *do* people manage those terrifying frame tents of great size and weight?) Peg the groundsheet at its corners, making the best use of the 'lie of the land' for comfort, making sure that in the event of rain it won't be flooded, and pointing the rear of it into the wind, if any. Insert the front pole in the loop at the apex of the inner tent (which is sewn to the groundsheet) and through the corresponding loop of the flysheet, and peg it erect with the guyline.

Repeat the process with the rear pole, and then peg the flysheet out all round. Adjust all pegs or guylines or both, according to the type of tent, so that they and the inner tent and the flysheet are taut but not tight, ensure that the flysheet stands well clear of the inner tent all round, and the dry and cosy outfit is ready for occupation.

Hardware like cooking stove and pans stays in the porch of the tent together with shoes, and food supplies are parked in the small space at the rear of the tent between it and the flysheet; there is rarely much that is perishable as that is eaten on the day of purchase as a rule. Sleeping bag, clothing and cycle bags go inside the tent as soon as it is erected, to avoid dampness.

There is almost always some condensation inside a small tent. The amount increases as the difference increases between the temperature outside and inside the tent, so that some ventilation which will help to equalise these is helpful in reducing it. Many tents have a small zipped opening or a small net grille for this purpose.

The exterior of the flysheet often gets very wet overnight, so the striking of the tent is left until last so that any morning sun can have the maximum drying effect – as it did the next morning at Arrochar. Having gone through the pitching procedure in reverse and repacked, I cycled back to Loch Lomond and northwards to Crianlarich, flanked by Ben Lui and Ben More, 3,708 and 3,843 ft. high (1,131 and 1,172 m). The small railway station here has a buffet which can usually provide food and drink.

Through Bridge of Orchy and round Rannoch Moor to Ballachulish the landscape became very barren; perhaps the thought of the 1692 massacre in Glen Coe made that valley seem especially so.

Ferries play an important part in communications in Scotland, and my first use of one from Ballachulish to North Ballachulish put me on the road to Fort William. Here I used the official camping site a little way up Glen Nevis, near Ben Nevis, the highest mountain in the British Isles at 4,406 ft. (1,336 m).

It rained that night, and I was again glad that I had a
tent which can be carried wet without deterioration; it's a
bit heavier when wet and has to be put in a waterproof
bag, but apart from that slight inconvenience all is well.
Camping is one of those things which is actually better in
practice than theory; even in bad weather it is convenient
and good fun providing one is well equipped.

There is a good minor road from near Fort William to
Loch Lochy, and I always take such roads in preference
to major roads even when the latter are relatively quiet,
as they were in Scotland at this time. By Loch Lochy I
came upon the youth hostel of that name and thought it
might be a good idea to camp at the hostel – it makes a
change, and the hostel facilities are useful from time to
time. A quick look at the Scottish Y.H.A. handbook,
however, revealed that camping is not permitted at any
hostels in that country; I wondered why. Still, that was
one thing less to think about and I ended up at a splendid
spot on the banks of Loch Ness near Drumnadrochit
instead. It was an athletic feat to reach the water in the
burn, but somehow I managed. Perhaps the proximity of
the burn accounted for the abundance of midges that
evening; fortunately they don't worry me too much but
for the many people who do get attacked it is advisable to
pitch camp well away from water, about which midges
congregate.

Daily mileages had so far been modest, but the next
day I pitched my tent 109 miles on, at the northern end
of Loch Stack. I had come through Inverness over the
ferry to Kessock and along to Conan Bridge and Dingwall,
up and over to Bonar Bridge, on to Lairg and along the
lengths of Lochs Shin, a Ghriama, Merkland and More to
Loch Stack. Here, on a little promontory, with the
mountains reflected in the waters of the loch, my tent
looked very tiny indeed.

Perhaps that sounds rather a long ride; it was in fact

longer than intended, for the last 15 miles were spent
looking for a camp site. Although there was plenty of
open land, most of it was wet and peaty; but in the end I
found a patch of springy turf. It was a day when
conditions were agreeable and a long ride enjoyable – it is
all a matter of how one feels at the time, of riding within
one's capacity, and of enjoying oneself.

A following wind had helped, but a breeze makes it
difficult to get good results from a little stove – and I
have a strict rule never to cook inside the tent, it is too
easy to have a serious accident! Eventually my tea was
brewed, and the chops brought with commendable
foresight from Inverness, with vegetables and sweet
course and cheese, disposed of. There had been no
opportunity to purchase supplies for the last 50 miles.

Now came the 40 miles to Cape Wrath. The first 25 or
so were on the A838, a winding, hilly road, and so
narrow that it had frequent bays for passing vehicles. It
leads to Keoldale on the Kyle of Durness, which is crossed
by a ferry boat to the lonely pier on the Cape Wrath
headland.

Ten minutes after my arrival at the ferry, I was hailed
by two other cyclists approaching – Mark and Jack, last
seen in Glasgow, who had made their way there by an
entirely different route! Low tide, and very little water in
the Kyle, seemed to me to mean that there would be a
long wait before the ferry could run, but after a while it
came over from the other side by a tortuous channel
which is navigable at all times: it is only a tiny boat with
an outboard motor; a couple of bikes and their riders
more than fill it – and the ferryman told me that it was
used by a large number of cyclists in the course of a year.

The 11 miles on the other side to Cape Wrath lighthouse are over a hilly, winding and very narrow road
with grass growing down the middle. The only motor

vehicles to use it are a Land Rover which takes supplies to the lighthouse and a public minibus which had broken down at the time. A brief glimpse of sunshine favoured my arrival at the cape, but on the return ride to the ferry I rode through heavy rain and a thunderstorm, passing Mark and Jack on the way.

By the time I reached the village of Durness on the mainland it was such a fine evening that I changed my plan to sleep under a roof for a change that night and instead pitched my tent on the top of the cliffs, a wonderful spot. It was broad daylight till almost 11 p.m. when it was still fine, but an hour or so later a high wind and heavy rain started. It was still the same in the morning, so it was a case of getting up and away as quickly as possible. It had been a good test for the tent, which remained quite dry inside, and perhaps a good test for its occupant as well.

Not least, such conditions are a test for the bicycle. Very heavy or continuous rain washes the oil from the chain and from the pedal bearings, which protest with grinding noises. A little lubrication is essential, and, when the weather is dry again, the chain should be wiped dry and oiled.

There are few houses and fewer shops in the north of Scotland, but there are occasional hotels along the roads and at most ferry crossing points around the coast. They seem quite accustomed to receiving bedraggled cyclists and provide hot drinks and food at all hours of the day. Such an hotel was at Rhiconich, 14 miles from Durness.

After negotiating the wild coast road from Laxford Bridge through Scourie to Kylestrome, the hotel at Kylesku served me equally well, and on my way southward under the gaunt outline of Quinag mountain I exchanged a cheery word with a large group of cycle tourists heading north.

Another series of 'A' roads about ten feet wide which lurched up and down among the lochs and glens were traffic-free and took me to Ullapool, a pleasant fishing town on Loch Broom, where several other cyclists had decided to halt for the night. For once, I really did sleep under a roof at Ullapool, and I dreamed of my cosy tent.

Going along Loch Broom and up to the Corrieshalloch Gorge the next day I began another lengthy ride which continued through Strathmore to Garve, then west through the heart of the Highlands – bleak and breezy – to Achnasheen, Achnashellach and Stromeferry (where there is no ferry). This area seemed to offer good possibilities for camping, so at Achmore, seeing a forester just finishing his day's stint, I bade him good evening and confided to him that I was looking for a few square feet of springy turf, hard by a clear burn, and amid some small trees for shelter from the wind. He thought for a few moments. 'Take the left turn down there,' he said, 'and go down the glen for half a mile; you'll find such a spot on your left, and you will not be disturbed, I assure you!' It was a grand spot.

Next day was Sunday, a quiet day in Scotland when few shops open. I was lucky to find one at Dornie which opened at eleven o'clock 'for the papers', at which I was able to stock up with provisions. It seemed the longest climb of the tour to reach 1,000 ft. (305 m) from sea level at Invershiel to the top of Glen Shiel (but it wasn't) from which point the snow line at about 3,000 ft. (915 m) was clearly visible on the mountains to the north.

From the western end of Loch Cluanie a road hoists itself over Glen Loyne and then descends to the northern end of Loch Lochy, along whose shores I spun over the only piece of road to be covered twice on the tour. A good little private camping site near Roy Bridge in Glen Spean made another convenient stopping place – with a view of the Ben Nevis massif from the tent.

It was near Loch Moy the next morning that I met Paul, regarding a flat tyre on his cycle with some dismay. Also a cycle-camper on tour, he had already used his spare tyre, so all we could do was to replace the one which had just burst with the much-patched old one which he had luckily kept. No chance of getting another before Perth, so we just rode on and hoped for the best, having made sure that the tyre with most tread was on the rear wheel. Even with the load distributed front and rear of the cycle as Paul's was, the rear tyre wears much faster than the front one as the drive is through the back wheel.

At Loch Laggan, we turned south at Laggan Bridge to Dalwhinnie, over a memorable high spot offering us a last snowy glimpse of the Ben Nevis range to the west. Dalwhinnie and the pass of Drumochter we found less interesting and dramatic that we had anticipated. The road is wide and quite out of sympathy with the countryside, and carries a good deal of traffic. Still, it provides a gentle rise to the summit of the pass at 1,504 ft. (458 m) and a fine swoop down to Blair Atholl and Pitlochry.

For the rest, it was a ride to Perth for the quick fitting of a new tyre on Paul's cycle – just in time, by the look of the old one! – and on to Edinburgh. Most of this ride was on the main road, but for much of the way a motorway takes most of the traffic to the benefit of the cyclist. The countryside by Kinross and Cowdenbeath was unexpectedly pleasant, in compensation for the disappointment a day or two before.

My keen sense of pleasant anticipation had been fully justified. Repacked for travelling order, my bags and cycle were loaded on the train at Edinburgh for the journey home. I had seen quite a bit of Scotland, but there was a lot unseen, especially the western islands and the north-east. I mentally began to plan the next tour there, as the train carried me back to England.

In the Pyrenees

We had travelled to Paris by the day rail/sea service and had the usual few hours to spend in the French capital before the departure of the overnight train to Biarritz – readily accessible by rail and a good starting point for our two-week exploration of the Pyrenees. We were four: John, Pete, Geoff and I. Geoff had not met the others before.

We dined in Paris with a French cyclist and his family and during the meal one of them asked Geoff how he could arrange to go on tour with people he had never met. 'That's easy – they're cyclists!' was the unhesitating reply – and of course by now Geoff had to all appearances known everyone for a long time. It doesn't take long for cyclists to break the ice.

On arrival at Biarritz the following morning we were dismayed to find that our cycles had not been put on the train by which we had travelled, and our first enquiries could elicit no information about their probable arrival time. We had heard of occasional instances where cyclists and their machines had become separated in this way, but it was the first time it had happened to us in our considerable experience of travelling with our cycles.

There was nothing for it but to resign ourselves to at least a day and a night in Biarritz, which turned out to be an agreeable resort, less sophisticated than we had imagined. We found accommodation at an hotel near the station; the rooms and food were good and there was a memorable toilet installation bearing the date 1889 – and it worked! During the day we made frequent enquiries at the station for news of our cycles, the station staff being helpful and telephoning round in an effort to locate them.

Next morning we were overjoyed to find that the cycles had arrived and lost no time in strapping our bags on them and wheeling away in the hot sunshine of late June. Heading south-eastwards through the valley of the river Nive we found (not for the first time) that a valley road is not necessarily a flat one, and we met three other cyclists from England coming the other way who were also confirming the fact. They were just finishing their tour and were able to tell of the delights which awaited us.

Here is the country of the Basques, who have a language of their own which is unrelated to any other European tongue. They also speak French, and everywhere play a local ball game called *pelota* which looks terrifyingly fast and far more strenuous than cycling.

The valley road after Cambo-les-Bains becomes narrower and carries little traffic though it is still well surfaced – typical, in fact, of very many of the roads in the Pyrenees – to reach St. Jean-Pied-de-Port, where there are some fine 16th and 17th century houses. On the Michelin map this road is edged with a green line, indicating a route through especially attractive countryside. A very large proportion of the roads in the Pyrenees are so marked, with every justification.

From St. Jean, we turned eastwards to tackle the Col d'Osquich, a comparatively modest summit at 1,280 ft. (392 m) – a road height not uncommon in Britain and providing just a foretaste of the climbing to come later in the tour. The descent to Mauleon was exhilarating, and by evening we had reached Tardets-Sorholus, having noted that a youth hostel was situated at nearby Montory. The hostel proved to be part of a small estate of prefabricated buildings just outside the village of

Montory. The estate looked incongruous and it was not until later that we learned that it replaced old buildings destroyed in an earthquake a few years before and not as yet fully rebuilt.

Much of the interest in youth hostelling is the great variety of buildings which are used as hostels – anything from castles to cottages. This one, although temporary, was comfortable and adequately equipped and although we were the only visitors that night, the *Livre d'Or* in the common room showed that it received many hostellers in the course of a year, including a number from Britain, some of whom had added complimentary remarks about the hostel.

The key to the hostel is kept by a lady living nearby, who tells you that the baker also sells potatoes and that he will tell you where milk may be obtained. But cyclists' appetites needed more than these 'basics' and it was John who volunteered to return the 4 kilometres to Tardets for supplies. He returned in quick time with a large supply of provisions. After all, we *had* covered 75 miles (120 km) which, as it turned out, was the longest day of the whole tour.

Next day, the sun had given way to wet and stormy conditions, but they did not deter us from riding up the quiet valley of the Aspe through magnificent mountain scenery to the Col du Somport at 5,380 ft. (1,632 m) on the borders of France and Spain. Soon after the summit the driving rain forced us to take shelter for a short time before resuming the descent. This was soon interrupted again by a little mechanical trouble with Geoff's free-wheel, to which he gave expert attention in the rain – the droll part of it was that the storm here was a very local one and we could see that a couple of miles either way and we would have been in hot sunshine!

The sort of thing you can laugh about afterwards? We couldn't help laughing at the time.

At Jaca, former capital of the kingdom of Aragon, we stopped for the night after 61 miles. We had not booked accommodation in advance at all, but here we found a splendid little hotel where the dinner was aptly described by Pete as a 'gastronomic experience'. Evening meals are taken somewhat later in Spain than we are accustomed to at home (from about 8.30 p.m. onwards) but are worth waiting for. Unusually, covered accommodation for the cycles was not available here; no cyclist can sleep well in the knowledge that his machine is exposed to the elements overnight, so we stowed the four of them in one of our rooms which happened to be on the ground floor.

We made short work of the 19 miles (30 km) to Biescas early the following morning. There we booked in at another small hotel and deposited our bags so that we could travel light for a look at the nearby Ordesa National Park. There is no road through the park so it is necessary to enter and leave it by the same road through Torla. What we hadn't realised was that there is a 4,650 ft. (1,423 m) col between Biescas and Torla, but with a few days riding already behind us and the advantage of little luggage to carry, this proved no obstacle. The winding road up the col, lined with wild roses, honey-suckle, clover and other wild flowers in abundance, and the sight of the canyon-like valleys and the mountains of the Monte Perdido range, more than repaid the effort involved. The undisturbed sights, scents and sounds as experienced from a bicycle are always beyond price.

Breakfast comes a bit late, too, in Spain, so it was 9.30 or so before we were on the road, our hotel bill having been tastefully made out to 'Senor Geoffrey and Familia'. But we reached the summit of the Portalet, and crossed there into France again, by 1 p.m. and sped down to les Eaux-Chaudes in hot sunshine. Geoff and I stopped here and exchanged looks. No words were needed for us to

understand that we both felt hungry, and that a slap-up
meal was called for rather than our usual picnic lunch.
John and Pete didn't need much persuasion, so we
invaded a restaurant and partook of five generous courses
each. After which, we all felt very much better, but oddly
enough unlike cycling a great distance. At Eaux-Bonnes,
not far down the road, at the foot of the Aubisque pass,
we called it a day, leaving the conquest of the pass until
the morrow.

Everywhere there was great interest in us as touring
cyclists – perhaps the greater because we were now in
Tour de France country although not in the least trying
to emulate the athletic feats of riders in that great event –
and the *patron* of the hotel we chose in Eaux-Bonnes was
particularly interested to know that we were to climb the
Aubisque. 'I ride to the top most mornings, as training
for winter sports,' he said. 'But of course I have no bags
on my cycle.' And he told us that it was misty up there
that day, so it was as well that we had deferred our
crossing for a day.

The crossing was not without incident. John had eaten
not wisely but too well. One of his brake cables snapped.
Geoff managed to break his chain on the way up.
Recovery from all these little delaying factors was rapid,
and we all agreed that the Aubisque was the finest pass
we had yet seen. The road summit is at 5,610 ft. (1,709 m)
and from it there is a magnificent panorama of jutting
mountain peaks rising a further 3,000 ft. (1,015 m). We
enjoyed the climb and the great reward at the top, and
were loth to leave.

A glance at a map of the Pyrenees will show at once the
lack of direct east-west roads affording any route through
the mountains which will give a proper appreciation of
them, and that to obtain this a circuitous tour is
essential. A visit to the Pyrenees will show how few
people make such a tour.

In order to continue in fine unfrequented country yet
fit in a visit to Lourdes, we decided to descend the
Ouzon valley and turn at Asson to the Gave de Pau (*gave*
is a word peculiar to the Pyrenees meaning a mountain
stream), visit the caves at Betharram and continue into
Lourdes. The main road south leads only to summer and
winter resorts and is not busy, the only through routes
being over the Col du Tourmalet, 6,933 ft. (2,115 m),
which we accordingly climbed the next day and over an
even higher col to the south.

This is one of the higher passes which are snow-bound
for most of the year; the Tourmalet is normally open only
between July and September. We were there early in
July and it was clear of snow, though as usual much extra
clothing had to be donned for the descent from the
summit, which was very cold for the first few miles. On
the way up Geoff had confessed that he'd 'never known
kilometre posts so far apart', and he had also observed
that 'every third house is a bar' – but then houses are a
long way apart in those mountains. Perhaps it was
because it was his twenty-first birthday that day;
anyway, we had all recovered sufficiently to celebrate the
occasion in suitable fashion that evening in Arreau.

Horseflies proved a bit troublesome the following day
as we rode in hot sunshine the 47 miles over the cols de
Peyresourde and du Portillon to Bosost (in Spain again)
and Viella. It was one of those days when the carrying
capacity of one's cycle bags is tested, as they have to
carry everything except shoes, socks and shorts. There
was a youth hostel shown on the map and in the guide at
Salardu, and as the villages along the little road became
smaller and smaller we hoped very much that the hostel
existed. After some searching, we found it and there were
signs of occupation – but no sign of anyone around the
place at all. The 'Marie Celeste' hostel we called it, and
after waiting as long as our appetites permitted to no

avail, we got fixed up instead at a simple but spotless hotel nearby.

A rough but rideable 14 miles (22 km) the next morning took us over the Puerto de la Bonaigua, a high track winding up to 6,800 ft. (2,072 m) through the sierra. On this short stretch of 'rough stuff' I managed to collect the only puncture of the tour – and that just a few yards from the point where we rejoined the metalled road down to Llavorsi.

It is difficult to imagine 30 miles of downhill roads, but here indeed was such a descent on a bicycle; apart from a few very short humps it was a freewheel all the way to Pobla de Sequi – the approach to that town being through the Desfiladero de Collegats, a long, deep gorge through hills of a crazy chaos of multi-coloured rocks, the faulted strata forming many varied patterns. It doesn't do to carry on downhill for such a long way without stopping. For one thing, you miss a chance to take in the scenery decently. For another, you get only one sweeping sensation instead of a succession of them. And finally it is wise to err on the side of caution and stop for a few minutes now and again to allow the rims to cool off; a lot of braking will cause them to heat up – they will be too hot to hold – and although the risk of tyre burst as a result is remote, it is better to eliminate the risk completely.

Looking at the map in Pobla that evening, the ride to Seo de Urgel by way of Tremp did not look too hard, although there are two climbs to around the 4,500 ft. (1,370 m) mark, at Faidella and Boixols. The view from the latter summit was one of the best of the tour – over the mountains of the Aigues Tortes national park with a backdrop of several 9,000 ft. (2,745 m) peaks.

At Seo de Urgel the hotel had a cyclist proprietor who had been to England, and he knew all about the

appetites which cyclists acquire after 65 hilly miles, as
well as the sustenance needed for tackling more of them
next day, which was to prove the high spot of the tour in
more ways than one.

The 13-mile (20 km) ride into Andorra, the capital of
the tiny state of the same name, was easy. The town is a
very popular tourist centre, full of gift shops and other
'attractions', all of which can be had much nearer home if
you like that sort of thing. We didn't, so after a brief stay
we took the steep mile or two to Encamp, after which
there is a short stretch of easier gradient before the start
of the Port d'Envalira road.

This is a climb of 13 miles (20 km) marked 12% (or 1
in 8). A huge hairpin with mile-long sides precedes
Soldeu, after which there are a straight few miles before
you start on the shorter hairpin bends which take you
above the tree line, up to the snow line and, on our day,
into the cloud line – which can be very much lower – at
the 7,900 ft. (2,405 m) summit height. Anoraks and 'longs'
were worn for the first part of the drop through the damp
mist, and even socks came in useful as gloves. The
temperature rapidly increases as height is lost, however,
and we were soon back to something like normal attire!

The border into France is crossed soon after the summit
of the Envalira, and after 22 miles (36 km) Spain is
re-entered at Bourg-Madame. Just here is an area which
was split between France and Spain two hundred years
ago, and the Spanish village of Llivia is still isolated in
French territory. We stayed at nearby Puigcerda, where
the good lady at the hotel was interested in our exploits
and told us that she had quite a lot of cyclist visitors
from abroad.

In the eastern Pyrenees the mountains are less high,
more wooded and have more cultivated valleys than in
the west. The ride over the Puerto de Tosas was very

fine, the climb to the 5,900 ft. (1,800 m) summit not being hard going though our small chainrings and large rear sprockets were much appreciated yet again. The way down the other side to Ripoli was through hills golden with broom on a winding road giving splendid views at every turn. We liked the mountain township of Camprodon, where we decided to spend our last night in Spain – the penultimate night of the tour.

Up from Camprodon to the Collado de Aros, where we entered France again, many miles downhill to Amelie-les-Bains, up steeply, then a succession of undulations to the Col Xatard – at a mere 2,500 ft. (762 m) – and then a descent to Boule, a tiny village boasting just one *pension*. at which we spent the night.

There is an easy way from Boule to Perpignan (where our ride was to end) and a hard way. For once there was some slight disagreement among the quartet about which way to go. Those in favour of the hard way prevailed, and the decision was not regretted, for after climbing into the hills again we descended on the eastern side where there is an amazing panorama of the end of the Pyrenean range with its foothills decreasing in size and rolling away to a narrow plain, with the Mediterranean beyond.

We cycled out to the coast at Canet to complete the ride from Atlantic to Mediterranean, and for the last few miles northward into Canet were confronted with a stiff headwind, very warm but very strong, which reduced our speed quite as much as had the 1 in 8's.

We had covered 750 miles awheel, spanning the range of mountains which are just 250 miles from end to end in a straight line. We were not interested in straight lines; in no other way could we have seen so much, had so many and varied experiences and enjoyed ourselves so much – and that's what holiday cycling is all about.

The cycles, registered from Perpignan to Paris and

thence to London, arrived when we did and were ready to be ridden home a few minutes after arrival in London. By the same service several other cyclists returned from their continental tours, including three who had been in the Pyrenees at the same time as we had. But we had not seen them there, and theirs is another story.

Ten in Somerset

We reached Somerset by various means. Three lads, Tom, Ralph and Harold, had arrived at Yarde by car, their cycles mounted on a roof rack. John had come from Derby by the same means, and so had Len from Tadworth – but he had parked the vehicle 10 miles away and completed the distance pedalling through the lanes. From Eastbourne, Fred had sought the help of British Railways, leaving himself a 20-mile potter to his destination. The lucky ones with more time to spare were Ken and Frances arriving by tandem from Godstone, having spent several days wheeling through the south country; Chris, who had cycled more rapidly to reach Yarde in two days from Haverhill; and I, who had taken the train to Salisbury and spent a leisurely two days riding down by way of Wells.

That ride from Salisbury is worth a mention in itself. There is a gorgeous little lane winding away from the centre of Salisbury to Quidhampton which is a typical quiet exit from a busy centre of the kind which can always be found by the cyclist with a little bit of perseverance. It is followed by a very short distance on a high-decibel main road before one dives into the Wylye valley along a lane where the cyclists outnumber the motorists (it was four and two respectively) for the best part of 10 miles after which the lanes thread out of Wiltshire and into Somerset – Sutton Veny, Longbridge Deverill, Upton Noble, Westcombe and Evercreech – it is

unlikely that many people other than cyclists have ever
heard of these hidden, charming villages.

Wells is busy but deserves attention before skilful
mapreading is needed to navigate a way across part of the
north Somerset plain – farming, peat cutting, irrigation
ditches – to Bridgwater and the hill country beyond.
Yarde lies to the north-west of the Quantock hills, a
finely shaped and well-wooded but small range of hills
north of Taunton, and our descent upon the hamlet in
such numbers almost doubled its population for a week.

Even before the first of our evening dinners – very
substantial meals, with large quantities of vegetables and
fruit all grown within yards of the table – we were all
chatting away like old friends; though we were not all in
the 'dedicated' class of cyclist – indeed, it was Fred's first
trial of a cycling holiday – we all had the same wish to
leave the world behind for a short time and enjoy a
carefree bumble about the countryside utterly
independent of conventional but needless trappings.

Our freedom was not even limited by a set programme
of rides each day. There is a lot to be said for flexibility,
and deciding where to go and what to do day by day; it
is the only way in which our English weather and the
inclinations of those concerned can be fully taken into
account. The inclinations of the territory to be explored
have a bearing on it, too. In the event we got ourselves
warmed up the first day by taking an up-and-down route
to Kilve and the lane which climbs up from there to the
Quantocks ridge. After a mile and two gates the lane
becomes a track, and soon after that a path which enters a
wood and becomes stony, so that even those few fit
people who had remained in the saddle this far were
brought down to earth to walk awhile.

It is an affront to such glorious countryside to move
through it too quickly and good to pause from time to

time – only thus, thereabouts, might you catch sight of a deer, a fox, or perhaps even a spotted woodpecker.

Abruptly the wood ended and we burst upon open moorland covered with heather and bracken; sunshine, breeze and a view extending across to Exmoor, the coast of north Somerset and over the Bristol Channel to south Wales. All this with fine cloud formations, indicated a stop for photography, a good excuse for a breather after climbing over half-way to the ridge track at about the 1,000 ft (305 m) level.

You have to be careful with the mapreading on that ridge track; or perhaps it is just that the views and the general experience of a heady feeling of wellbeing impair ability, but it is easy to take the wrong path even in such a limited area. The secret is not to lose height; if you find yourself doing so, retrace at once. John and Chris learned this by experience as I had somehow forgotten to tell them that I had been that way before – and knew they were going wrong, some distance ahead.

The idea was to get to a certain hostelry in time for a drink and a bite before closing time. So heady were we already that closing time – 2 p.m. – had just passed when we arrived; our 15 miles in some four hours did not indicate any sense of urgency about things. So we had our own ploughman's lunch, and brewed our tea, at Crowcombe before ambling back to Stogumber and 'home'. Just 23 miles, which goes to prove that you can't measure cycling enjoyment in miles. A mile on a cycle is usually at least five minutes of uniquely pleasurable experience, but on this day each one had been more like twenty keenly enjoyed minutes. A day which went to show, among other things, how manageable in such country a tandem and a wife can be, for Ken got them both round without demur, and without a scratch on the frame of either. Frances was a good stoker, but the characteristic of a tandem is always that although much faster than a solo machine on descents it is slower when climbing.

The next day, after a look at the finest remains of monastic buildings in the south-west at Cleeve Abbey, near Washford, we rode through the Druid's Combe to Luxborough, where there is a pub which is always ready to serve wayfarers with coffee, especially when they are a bunch of bedraggled cyclists – had I mentioned that it was a very wet day, and that we were enjoying ourselves no end? 'Tell me when you're coming this way again, and I'll arrange to swim the channel that day!' was Ralph's comment. But we were well equipped with waterproofs which kept us dry underneath.

Up and over to Dunster – yarn market, castle, very pleasant village – followed by a smart run along the coast to Watchet, and we were left with only a few miles to cover back to base.

'I thought low gears were ridiculous when I first saw your tiny chainring,' someone said to me. 'But I am beginning to see what you meant when you said that it isn't used much but it's nice to know that it's there!' The fact is that the hills in the south-west of England – as elsewhere in the country – are quite often steeper than continental ones, which although in many cases are very much longer are engineered to keep the gradient reasonable – the difference between 1 in 8 or 10 and the 1 in 4 or 6 pitches here. Many times we found ourselves running through the gears rapidly from top to bottom at the foot of these short, steep climbs, and changing back into top again as soon as we reached the summit.

Low gears are useful in other circumstances. They ensure full control of the cycle on level ground when it is wet or slippery. One day we went over to Dulverton and returned along a 5-mile bridleway through the valley of

the river Haddeo in Hartford Bottom, and this
September, after a very wet summer, the going for much
of the way was very muddy. I recalled this valley as a
most attractive meander off the beaten track which I had
enjoyed several times in warm sunshine, and although
nothing could detract from its beauty, the conditions
underfoot on this occasion were bad and low gears the
order of the day. The river was in spate and had to be
crossed at one point – we were just getting ready to wade
it when we spotted a rickety, narrow bridge not far
upstream.

What sort of people are they who decide, quite
independently of one another, that this is the holiday for
them? This group was typical: a couple of ex-miners, an
insurance official and a business man (all of them in
retirement, well over sixty years of age – the latter with
his wife), a banker, a development engineer (the baby of
the party at thirty), a metalworker, an export manager
and a schoolmaster.

Our host Alf, a septuagenarian, dusted off his
Sunbeam bicycle (twenty years his junior) and took us
out the next day. After a look at Nettlecombe Court, an
old manor house now used as a field study centre, we
ambled on to Monksilver and Sampford Brett, where for
local history and information the church provides the
best source. Fortunately, quiet and lovely places like
these do not find their way into guide books.

On to the little port of Watchet for elevenses and then
we traced the route of the former West Somerset Mineral
railway, abandoned half a century ago. Somewhere along
this track there crossed an even older one, used by
monks centuries earlier on their way from Cleeve Abbey
to the coast, and an ancient stone bridge over the
Washford river nearby has a cross which was carved on
the central stone by them.

Time to imagine past scenes whilst the tandem was upturned, a puncture in the rear tube located and repaired – unless you were helping with the repair, that is; it is arguable whether many hands make light work on these occasions, but there was no shortage of hands and advice.

Why take the broad highway when you can take a deserted lane through rolling country through Withycombe to Carhampton, giving you an extra mile or two as an added bonus? You have all day. If you hurry, you won't see the fine screen in the church at Carhampton – or the fine pub sign at the house opposite, one of the several such signs in the district which are the work of a local artist.

Having a local 'guide' like Alf is a great help in getting to know an area. In a country like ours, there is so much to be seen in a small area that even with careful pre-planning and assiduous mapreading it is easy to miss a lot. The same applies to many places abroad, but wherever the cyclist goes he will not find the locals backward in offering local information or in telling him how to reach places of interest.

We probably would never have found the path along the sea shore into Minehead without Alf, and probably if he hadn't taken us that way, he would not have punctured either, but after a short delay (and something to eat) we turned our wheels towards Yarde to complete a 27-mile day full of interest and incident.

'I've never been to Cheddar,' said John next morning. 'Anyone coming?' A ride of some 70 miles, but more interest was shown when it was pointed out that for much of the way it was flat. But Fred had a similar wish to get to the top of Dunkery Beacon, in quite the opposite direction and although less than half the distance a very hilly ride. We decided to split up, four heading for Cheddar, six for Dunkery.

Making an early start for Minehead along the main road before the traffic was heavy, the hill-climbers warmed up by riding to the top of North Hill to the West and dropping by hillside paths to Selworthy, a thatched village owned by the National Trust, and so to Luccombe. Luccombe is about 400 ft. (122 m) above sea

Some cycle tourists are determined to reach the top . . .

level, and $2\frac{1}{2}$ miles on, at its nearest point to Dunkery Beacon, the road is at 1,450 ft. (441 m), after one of the hardest climbs for cyclists in the south-west; the notorious Porlock Hill is steeper but much shorter.

Even with a 25″ gear it is quite a push, and the sensible cyclist will take his bike for a walk on the last mile to the top, from where a rough track leads to the summit of the Beacon nearly a mile away. The exhilaration and extensive views on reaching the top are a great culmination of the slowly unrolling panorama of the ascent; not an isolated experience but the achievement of a continuous and wholly agreeable one.

It is quicker getting back – a rapid drop to Wheddon Cross, from where the road over the Brendon Hills climbs to over 1,000 ft. (305 m) and stays there for 11 miles (17·5 km), in the whole of which distance the only habitation is the inn at Ralegh's Cross, at which point we turned left for the final run downhill to our base.

Meantime the minority party had been to Bridgwater, found a way through the lanes to Cheddar, stopping for a picnic lunch at Westhay (lunch was taken in a barn as it was raining just then), seen the gorge and the caves and returned, finding in this direction that they hadn't got things all their own way. The wind prevails from the south-west in that part of the country, and their speed had been reduced by a rising breeze from that quarter; never mind, lower gears again came in useful, the thoughts of a huge dinner ahead spurred them on, and they arrived just as it was ready.

It is obvious that there are many hobbies, sports, recreations and games (cycling is all of these and more) which are followed by people from many walks of life and of widely differing ages. It is not so obvious that there is another one, apart from cycling, that attracts those from *every* walk of life and of every age from nine to ninety; age and occupation are quite irrelevant if you are a cyclist.

If cycle touring were just riding about, it would be impossible to explain this spirit which prevails among cyclists. It is explained by the attitude to life which is engendered by cycling, and which they share – the contentment of quiet progress through the countryside in the open air, the curiosity to find out what is round the corner or over the hill, the enjoyment of seeing new places and meeting new people, and the acceptance of good things and not-so-good, as they come. It is almost a way of life in itself, a placid philosophy which keeps convention and formality firmly in their place and sees the more material things for what they are worth. It is no longer surprising, then, that with these things in common, age and status also get in the right perspective.

But we are keeping our cyclists waiting to go for their last run which will take them to Wellington and the Blackdown Hills, southwards from Yarde, and so complete the boxing of the compass during the week. There is general lamenting that the time has passed so quickly and that the holiday is such a short one; much packing of bags for the return journeys and many exchanges of addresses, for the friendships just made will endure.

Then back to the everyday routine again. But after the adventure and relaxation of the week, and with the placid philosophy of the cyclist, that can be faced – until the next cycle tour.

12

Some suggested cycling tours

Here are some examples of actual cycling tours. Half an hour could be well spent with the appropriate map tracing some of the routes to see how the cyclist finds quiet, enjoyable riding of unflagging interest whilst taking in the popular cities, towns and attractions as well if he wishes. The times at which the well-known 'tourist' and sightseeing spots are busy are often predictable and avoidable by the cyclist without the handicap of a fixed timetable, and in towns he has an enviable mobility.

The tours may be made whole or in part (sections of the British ones form ideal weekend excursions) and they may be extended, curtailed or amended at will. They are intended as guides to the cyclist's practically unlimited scope for good times.

Approximate distances are shown in miles/kilometres thus: 10/16. Places of interest are not listed; they are far too numerous and should be selected according to individual inclination, hobby or study. Overnight stops have not been suggested as these too will depend upon personal fancy and the daily mileages envisaged.

The handbook of the Cyclists' Touring Club – which is sold to members only, but all cyclists should be C.T.C. members for the many ways in which it helps them – tourist office accommodation lists and the Y.H.A. Handbook between them give a wide choice of stopping places. Also listed in the C.T.C. handbook are the addresses of many members in Britain who act as honorary 'Local Information Officers'; they supplement the club's national touring service by offering to give local information and advice to fellow-members proposing to tour in their areas. The handbook does not list accommodation abroad.

The club's membership is world-wide and some members on the continent (and in other parts of the world) offer similar assistance to members contemplating tours in their countries.

Tour No. 1: Wessex
A circular tour from Winchester

Maps: Bartholomew's National Map Series 1:100,000, sheets 4 (Dorset), 5 (New Forest and Isle of Wight) and 7 (Bristol and North Somerset).

Winchester. Leave by A31, after 1/1·6 fork right: Pitt Down, Farley Down, Braishfield, Ganger Hill, Cupernham: rejoin A31 on outskirts of **Romsey** (13/21).

Leave Romsey by A3057 (Stockbridge road), after 1½/2 turn left on B3084 for 2/3·2 then turn left: Lockerley, East Dean, West Dean, East Grimstead; cross A36 to Alderbury, Britford, East Harnham, **Salisbury** (16/25·5). (Note that Salisbury is a good centre from which to spend several days exploring the valleys of the rivers Avon, Wylye, Ebble, Nadder and Bourne.)

Leave Salisbury by A345 (Amesbury road), soon after passing under railway bridge fork left to Woodford, Wilsford, West Amesbury: left on to A303 for 1/1·6 to **Stonehenge** (10/16).

Retrace on A303 through Amesbury, after 1/1·6 turn left: Bulford, Milston, Fittleton, Upavon; join A345 to **Pewsey**, then B3087 to Burbage, turn left on to A338 for 1/1·6 to Steep Green, turn right, after 1½/2 left through Grand Avenue, Savernake Forest to join A4 to **Marlborough** (10/16).

Leave Marlborough by A4 westwards, after 2/3·2 take

left to Lockeridge, Alton Priors, turn right to Allington, Horton, join A361 to **Devizes** (15/24).

Leave Devizes by A361, after 3/4·8 turn right on to A365 to Melksham (Lacock, 3/4·8 to north), A3053 Holt, Bradford-on-Avon, Limpley Stoke, **Bath** (20/32).

Leave Bath by A367 (Radstock road), after 3/4·8 turn left, Wellow, cross A366, Lullington, Oldford, turn right on to A361, to **Frome** (14/22·4).

Leave Frome by A362 to Warminster (passing Longleat), turn right on to A350, after 2/3·2 right to Maiden Bradley, cross B3092, Kilmington, (Stourhead estate), Stourton, then B3092/A303, Mere, turn right, Motcombe, **Shaftesbury** (24/38·4).

Leave Shaftesbury on B3091, on outskirts of town turn right: Todber, Marnhull, Stourton Caundle, Allweston, then A3030/A352 to **Sherborne** (18/28·8).

Retrace from Sherborne on A352, after 2/3·2 turn left: Totnell Corner, Minterne Magna, A352 to Cerne Abbas, turn right: Maiden Newton, Toller Porcorum, Powerstock, Bradpole, **Bridport** (27/43).

Leave town centre by road south to West Bay, then B3057: Swyre, Abbotsbury, turn right Langton Herring, Buckland Ripers, **Weymouth** (19/30·4).

Leave by A353 to Preston, left to Culliford Tree, **Dorchester**. Leave by A35 eastwards, after 2/3·2 turn right: Tincleton, Worgret, A352 **Wareham** (25/40).

Leave Wareham by A351 (Swanage road), after 1/1·6 right: Creech Heath, Church Knowle, Corfe Castle, Nine Barrow Down, **Swanage**, Studland, Haven Point – ferry to Sandbanks, **Bournemouth** (22/35).

Leave Bournemouth by A35 or B3059 to Christchurch, then B3059/A35 to Hinton Admiral (7/11 from centre of Bournemouth). Turn left to Thorney Hill, Burley, then right, cross A35 at Wilverley Post, then first left to **Brockenhurst** (19/30·4).

Leave Brockenhurst by A337 (Lymington road) after
1/1·6 turn left: Boldre, Lymington, Norleywood,
Beaulieu: take B3056 for 1/1·6 then turn right, Dibden
Bottom, Colbury, turn left for 1/1·6 to Lyndhurst Road
station (Lyndhurst 2/3·2), turn right, **Cadnam** (23/36·8).

Cross A36 to East Wellow, cross A27 to Newtown,
Lockerley, Mottisfont, Bossington church, Horsebridge,
Kings Somborne, Ashley, Pitt Down and back to
Winchester (24/38·4).

Total: 288/461.

Tour No. 2: The Cotswolds
A circular tour from Cirencester

Maps: Bartholomew's National Map Series 1:100,000,
sheets 13 (Hereford and Gloucester) and 14 (Oxford).

Leave Cirencester by A429 (Northleach road), after 1/1·6
turn right on to A433, after $1\frac{1}{2}$/2·4 turn right to
Quenington, where left to Coln St. Aldwyn, **Bibury**, Coln
Rogers, Coln St. Dennis, turn right (minor road) to
Northleach (17/27), Farmington, Sherborne, Windrush,
Great Barrington, Great and Little Rissington,
Bourton-on-the-Water, Bourton Bridge, **Lower and
Upper Slaughter**, Lower Swell, **Stow-on-the-Wold**
(19/30), Broadwell, Evenlode, **Moreton-in-Marsh**,
Batsford, Draycott, **Chipping Campden**, Broadway Hill,
Broadway (20/33), Snowshill, Temple Guiting, Guiting
Power, Charlton Abbots, Brockhampton, **Andoversford**
(18/28).

Leave on A436 (Gloucester road), after 1/1·6 turn left to
Withington, Cassey Compton, **Chedworth Roman Villa**,
Chedworth, Calmsden, North Cerney, turn left on to
A435, after $1\frac{1}{2}$/2·4 turn right, cross A417, Daglingworth,
Duntisbourne Rouse, Edgeworth, Miserden, Wishanger,

Lypiatt Park, **Stroud** (28/45).

Leave Stroud by A419 (Gloucester road), at Ebley
($1\frac{1}{2}$/2·4) turn left on to A46 and after $\frac{1}{2}$/0·8 right on
B4066. After $3\frac{1}{2}$/6 left to Nympsfield, Kingscote, left on
A4135 for $\frac{3}{4}$/1·2, then right to Newington Bagpath, cross
A46 at crossroads after 2/3·2 turn left to **Tetbury** (15/24).

Leave Tetbury by B4067, cross A433 to Cherington,
Tarlton, Coates (footpath to source of river Thames) and
join A419 to **Cirencester** (12/19).

Total: 129/205.

Tour No. 3: The wild Wales
Starting from Hereford and finishing at Shrewsbury

Maps: Bartholomews National Map Series 1:100,000,
sheets 13 (Wye Valley), 17 (Cardigan), 22 (Mid-Wales),
23 (North Shropshire) and 27 (North Wales).

Leave **Hereford** by A435 (Abergavenny road), after
2/3·2 turn right on to B4349, Gorsty Common, Coldwell,
join B4348 Vowchurch, Peterchurch (the Golden Valley),
Dorstone, **Hay-on-Wye** (20/32).

Leave Hay by A4153 northwards, at toll bridge after
3/4·8 take road to right to Brilley, Michaelchurch on
Arrow, Newchurch, mountain road to Glascwm,
Hundred House, where left on A481 to **Builth Wells**
(22/35).

Leave Builth by A483 (Llandovery road), after $\frac{1}{2}$/0·8
(immediately after crossing river bridge) turn right,
Llanvihangel Bryn Pabuan, turn right to Newbridge on
Wye, right on A479, after 300 yards left to Disserth, on
to A433 where turn left to **Llandrindod Wells** (13/21).

Continue on A483 to Cross Gates, after 3/1·8 left to
Abbey Cwmhir, mountain road to St. Harmon where turn
right on B4511 to **Llanidloes** (22/35).

Leave Llanidloes on B4518 to Clywedog reservoir, Bont-dolgadfan where turn left, Tal y Wern, join A489 to **Machynlleth** (26/42).

Leave Machynlleth by A487 (Dolgellau road), cross river at 3/1·8 then turn right on B4404 to Llanwrin, join

An expedition group off the beaten track in the hills of North Wales

A458 at Dinas Mawddwy. In village turn right to
Llanymanddwy, Bwlch y Groes (1,790 ft./540 m), Bryn,
Llangower (alongside Lake Bala) to **Bala** (35/56).

   Leave Bala by A494 (Corwen road), after 2/3·6 turn
right on to B4401 to Llandrillo, Cynwyd, join A5 at
Corwen. In village take lane to left and at T junction with
B5437 turn right. Follow this road in Dee valley to Rhewl
and **Llangollen** (24/39).

   Leave Llangollen by A539 to Ruabon, where turn right
(still on A539) to junction with A528, Overton, Ellesmere,
turn right by church to Lee, Bagley, Stanwardine-in-the-
Fields, Baschurch, Walford Heath, Leaton, **Shrewsbury**
(32/51).

Total: 194/311.

Tour No. 4: Suffolk and Norfolk

Ipswich to Norwich in a roundabout way.

Maps: Bartholomew's National Map Series 1:100,000,
sheets 21 (Suffolk) and 26 (Norfolk).

Leave **Ipswich** southwards on A137, after 2/3·2 turn left
on A138 to Freston, B1080, Holbrook, Stutton, rejoin
A137 for 2/3·2 then right on B1070 East Bergholt
(Constable country; Flatford Mill 3/1·6 south of E.
Bergholt) cross A12 to **Hadleigh** (20/32).

   Leave Hadleigh on B1070, after 2/3·2 left to Monks
Eleigh, **Lavenham**, lane via Acton to **Sudbury**; leave on
A131 (Halstead road) and after 1/1·6 turn right at
Ballingdon to Bulmer, Little Yeldham, Great Yeldham,
turn right on A604, after $\frac{1}{2}$/0·8 left to Stambourne,
Finchingfield (32/51).

   B1053 Great Sampford, B1054 Hempstead, Steeple
Bumpstead, B1057 **Haverhill**, A143 Little Wratting, left
at crossroads B1061, Little Thurlow, Great Bradley, turn

Cycle visitors to Europe from the United States

right Cowlinge, Lidgate, Ousden, Hargrave, Little
Saxham, **Bury St. Edmunds** (40/64).

Leave Bury St. Edmunds by A143 (Bungay road), after
1/1·6 right to Thurston, Pakenham, Stowlangtoft,
Badwell Ash, Walsham le Willows, turn left after 2/3·2,
cross A143, Hepworth, Barmingham, turn right B1111,
Garboldisham (23/37).

Cross A1066, take B1114 to Kenninghall, Old
Buckenham, **Attleborough**, cross A11, Great Ellingham,
Hingham, cross B1108 Thuxton, B1135 **East Dereham**,
leave on B1110 (Holt road) to North Elmham, right on
B1145 Bawdeswell, Reepham, Cawston, **Aylsham** (22/35).

Burgh, next Aylsham, Swanton Abbot, cross B1150,
Warstead, cross A149 Horning, East Ruston, Brunstead,
Ingham, Hickling (Hickling Broad), Catfield Common,
Catfield, cross A149, Horning (centre for Broads), turn
left for Horning ferry, Woodbastwick, New Backheath,
Norwich (38/61).
Total: 205/328.

Tour No. 5: Yorkshire Dales and moors
A circular tour from York

Maps: Bartholomews National Map Series 1 : 100,000,
sheets 32 (West Yorkshire), 35 (Darlington and North
Yorks), 36 (Teesside and Yorkshire Moors) and 33 (York
and Humberside).

Leave York by A59 (Harrogate road), and after 1/1·6 turn
left on to B1224 to Rufforth, Long Marston, where right
at crossroads, Tockwith, Cowthorpe, cross A1, turn right
on B6164 to Knaresborough, then A59 to **Harrogate**. (To
avoid A59, retrace 1/1·6 on B6164 from Knaresborough
and turn right for lane to Harrogate via Oatlands.) (21/33).

Leave centre of Harrogate by minor road to Oakdale,

cross B6161, go straight on ('Penny Pot Lane') to B6457, turn left, then after $\frac{1}{4}$/0·4 turn right to Fewston, past reservoir, left at T junction, right after 2/3·6 to Askwith, where right to Ilkley Bridge and **Bolton Bridge** (Wharfedale) (22/36).

B6160 to Bolton Abbey, fork right after $\frac{1}{4}$/0·4 to Appletreewick, Hartlington, Hebden, join B6265 to Grassington. Leave by minor road to Kettlewell, then B6160 to Buckden, Bishop Dale, Thoralby, **Aysgarth** (32/51).

Cross river Ure, turn left at Caperby to Woodhall, Askrigg, turn right over moor to Swaledale, turn left on B6270 to Muker (11/17). B6270 Thwaite, Keld, West Stones Dale, Tan Hill, moorland road to Arkengarth Dale, **Reeth** (20/31).

Leave Reeth by B6270, after 1/1·6 at Fremington straight on over moorland road to Marske, Richmond (lower Swale Dale), B6271 Catterick, Great Langton, **Northallerton** (16/25).

Leave Northallerton by minor road to Kirby, Jeater Houses, then left on A19 and after $\frac{1}{2}$/0·8 turn right to Thimbleby, Osmotherly. Retrace $\frac{1}{2}$/0·8 from Osmotherley, take first left up to Osmotherley Moor, follow moorland road to Hawnby, Rievaulx, **Helmsley** (22/35).

Leave Helmsley by A170 to Kirbymoorside (lane via Harome good alternative) where turn left to Hutton-le-Hole, Blakey Ridge, **Castleton** (22/35). (Note: At Little Blakey, at the summit of Blakey Ridge, this road crosses the trackbed of a long-disused railway. The surface is smooth: to the left it goes to Battersby – whence road to Kildale and Castleton – and to the right to Spaunton Moor near Rosedale Abbey, whence Cropton and Pickering.)

Danby, Glaisdale, Egton, Grosmont, Sleights, Ruswarp, **Whitby** (18/29).

Leave Whitby by lane to Whitby Laithes, High Hausker,

Fyling Thorpe, **Robin Hood's Bay**. From here, there is a
rough path past Boggle Hole to join road to Staintondale
and A171; alternatively, retrace to A171 at Evan Howe,
turn left to Penny Howe, where right into Harwood
Dale; Suffield Moor, Suffield, Hackness, Troutsdale,
Snainton (27/43).

Turn left on to A170 to Brompton, where turn right to
Sherburn, cross A64, Weaverthorpe, Kirby Grindalhythe,
North Grimston, **Malton** (20/32).

From Malton, minor road to Whitewall Corner,
Thornethorpe, Kirkham, left on A64 and after $\frac{1}{4}$/0·4 right
to Foston, Thornton le Clay, Strensall, Huntington, **York**
(20/32).

Total: 251/400.

Tour No. 6: France
Clermont Ferrand, some gorges, the Cevennes, Roman
towns and the Alps

Maps: Michelin 1:200,000 series, sheets 73, 76, 77, 80
and 81.

Leave **Clermont Ferrand** by N9 (le Puy road) and after
9/14 turn left on D225 to Vic-le-Comte; on to junction
with N496 where turn right to Sauxillanges and junction
with N499; St. Germain l'Herm, St. Alyre d'Ariane, la
Chaise-Dieu (66/106).

N106 Sambadel, Chamborne, N498 Crapanne-sur-
Arzon, D9 St. Georges-Lagricol, **Retournac** (29/46).

N103 Verey, Lavoute-sur-Loire, **Gorges de
Peyredevre**, le Puy; N589 Bains, Monistrol d'Allier
(Gorges d'Allier), Saugues, N585 Esplantas, Grandrieu,
Chateauneuf-de-Randon (55/88).

N88 Laubert, Pelouse, Mende, Balsieges; N586 then
D31 to Faux, N107 **Florac** (44/70).

N107, after $3\frac{1}{2}$/5·5 take N583, Barre-des-Cevennes, St. Jean-du-Gard, D153 Lasalle, Colognac, D185 Col de Readres, D133 St. Hippolyte-du Fort (55/88). N99 Sauve, Quissac, D35 Sommières, D40 Calvisson, **Nimes** (38/61).

N579 Pont St. Nicolas, Uzes, N582 St. Hippolyte-de-Montaigu, join D101 Pouzhilac, St. Victor-la-Coste, St. Laurent-des-Arbres, D26 Lirac, Tavel, **Avignon** (47/75).

N580 Sauveterre, Roquemaure, N576 **Orange** (16/25).

N575 Camaret, Vaison, N538 and after 2/3·5 take D54 Entrechaux, D13 and after 3/5 D40 St. Leger, Reilhanette, N542 Aurel, **Sault** (47/75).

N550 Revest-du-Bion, Banon, la Bastie, N551 St. Etienne-les-Orgues, Mallefougasse, D101 and N100 les Mées, Malijai, D8 **Digne** (61/97).

N100A la Javie, Beaujeu, join N100, Seyne-les-Alpes, Sélonnet, Espinasses; turn left on to N542 and after $5\frac{1}{2}$/9 N542A to Valserres, **Gap** (55/88).

N94 la Roche-des-Arnauds, after 5/8 turn right on to N537A, Montmaur, N517 Agnières, St. Disdier, les Barraques, les Payas, D66 Cordeac, St. Sebastien, D227, N526, N85 **La Mure** (50/80).

N529 la Motte d'Aveillans, Notre Dame de Commiers, Montchabond, Visille de Masage, D5 Eybens, **Grenoble** (30/48).

Total: 615/983.

Tour No. 7: Austria and Germany
Tyrol, Lakes, Bavaria

Maps: Holzel 1:200,000 Tyrol sheet; Deutsche Generalkarte 1:200,000, sheets 23 and 25/26 (combined in one sheet).

(Note: *Tal* – valley, *See* – lake.)

Some suggested cycling tours   234

Leave **Innsbruck** by minor road from north of city
eastwards to Rum, Terfens, Stans, Jenbach, where turn
right to cross river Inn by small bridge, left at main road,
then turn right after 1¼/2 into the Zillertal; Fügen,
Stumm, **Zell-am-Ziller** (40/63).

Turn left into Gerlostal; Gmünd, Gerlos Pass, Krimml,
Neukirch, Bramberg, Mühlbach, Mittersill; turn left on to
road 159, cross river Saalbach and after 1¼/2 turn right to
Stuhlfelden, Uttendorf, Piesendorf (Zell-am-See 2/3 to
north), **Bruck** (62/99).

St. Georgen, Taxenbach, Eschenau, turn left, Dienten,
Mühlbach, join road 159, **Bischofshofen** (38/60).

Road 159 to Werfen, Sulzau, then after 7/11 turn right
to Scheffau, Abtenau, after 2/3 turn left to Russbach,
Pass Gschütt, Gosaumühle, **Hallstatt** (44/70).

Round head of Hallstättersee, Obertraun, left on road
145 to **Bad Aussee**, turn right in town for Altaussee,
Rettenbachalm, Bad Ischl. Turn right on to road 145 to
Mittenweissenbach, Ebensee, lakeside road to **Gmunden**
(50/80).

Retrace to Altmünster, where turn right to
Neukirchen, Seefeld; turn right on road 152 for circuit of
the Attersee: Alexenau, Seewalden, Attersee, Parschallen,
Unterach (40/63).

Turn right to See, Loibichl, Mundsee, right at crossroads after ¾/1 to Zell, Strasswalchen, Markt. Turn right
on 157, after 2/3 turn left to Palting, cross main road,
Berndorf, Seeham, Obertrum and after ¾/1 turn right to
Elixhausen, **Salzburg** (50/80).

Leave Salzburg to north-west: Bergheim (Austria/
Germany frontier), Freilassing; turn right and after ¾/1
turn left to Schönram, Waging, Otting, Traunreut, Stein,
turn right to **Altenmarkt** (32/51).

Winter sunshine

Road 304 to Obing, Wasserburg; retrace $\frac{3}{4}/1$ and fork right to Griesstadt, turn right and cross river Inn to Schalldorf, Assling, Glonn, Putzbrunn, **München (Munich)** (42/67).
Total: 398/633.

Equipment lists

Here are some basic equipment lists for summer tours.
The principle is to take all that is needed, and nothing
that is not – if, on return from a tour, there are items in
the kit which have not been used, do not take them next
time. This applies to everything except tools and spares,
which should always be carried although rarely needed.

For a short tour (up to seven days)
Riding wear: Shorts, vest, shirt, short socks, shoes.
   Saddlebag only: 2 shirts, 2 sets underwear, 3 pairs
socks (1 long, 2 short), pullover (long sleeved),
lightweight trousers, plimsolls or sandals, toilet bag,
shaver or razor, towel, handkerchiefs, pyjamas.
   Side pockets: (1) First aid (including scissors and safety
pins, often useful). (2) Tools, lock and chain, puncture
outfit, 3 tyre levers, shoe cleaning kit.
   Strapped to top of bag: Cape, cap or 'sou'wester',
leggings. Approximate weight of saddlebag and contents
as above: 15 lb. (6·8 kg).
   Optional extras: Swim trunks, camera, sunglasses, tie,
sewing kit ('housewife'), suntan lotion, insect repellent,
notebook/biro, zip jacket or anorak.
   For winter riding, some extra garments will probably
be needed, for example 'plusses', a complete track suit or
windcheater and long trousers; but remember that
cycling soon gets the circulation going and that body
warmth is a result of this and not external heat. It is easy
to wear too much even in winter and to get
uncomfortably warm. Gloves are a necessity in cold
weather, however.

For a longer tour, extra sets of underwear and outer garments will be required, and these should be packed as neatly as possible, adding pannier bags, or using them instead of a saddlebag, according to need.

For a summer camping tour

Riding wear: as above.

Saddlebag: Tent (groundsheet sewn in), flysheet, pegs and guys; filled sleeping bag, plimsolls or sandals, toilet bag, towel, dish cloth, drying cloth.

Side pockets: (1) $\frac{1}{2}$-pt. primus stove, puncture outfit, 3 tyre levers, tin opener, matches, lock and chain. (2) Tools, cup, shoe cleaning kit.

Strapped to top of bag: as above.

Pannier bags: (1) 2 shirts, 2 sets underwear, 3 pairs socks (1 long, 2 short), pullover (long sleeved), lightweight trousers, handkerchiefs, pyjamas. (2) Set of cooking pans, food containers, knife, fork, spoons (dessert and tea), plate, space for food.

Pannier side pockets: (1) First aid kit, toilet paper. (2) Priming fuel for stove, extra bottle (aluminium) for water or paraffin (but not for both).

If the tent will not fit in the saddlebag as suggested, it may go into a pannier bag, and the items listed for the latter carried in the saddlebag. If the tent is too big for either, it should be strapped along or across the rear pannier carrier, where in any case the tent poles should be carried if they do not fit in the seat tube of the cycle.

Remember that the tent will be the first thing required on arrival at the camping site, so it should be readily accessible. Tools and first-aid should also always be carried where they can be reached without delay.

The weight of the camping and touring equipment – including any of the optional extras – should not exceed 30 lb. (13·6 kg). Ladies should substitute their equivalent garments in the above lists; their load may be a little lighter!

Tools

The following should always be carried: puncture outfit with 3 tyre levers, spare gear cable, spare brake cables, spanner(s) to fit all nuts, screwdriver, oil in leakproof container.

These further tools should also be carried on long tours or on tours where assistance is unlikely to be obtainable: spare inner tube, spare brake blocks, spare lamp bulbs and batteries, spare spokes, spoke key, chain rivet extractor, spare links for chain, small pliers, spare cotter pin (if using cottered cranks), supply of rag.

Puncture!

Official National Tourist offices in London

Austria	Austrian State Tourist Department 16 Conduit Street, W1
Belgium	Belgian National Tourist Office 66 Haymarket, SW1
Bulgaria	Bulgarian National Tourist Office 126 Regent Street, W1
Cyprus	Cyprus Tourist Centre 213 Regent Street, W1
Czechoslovakia	Czechoslovak Travel Bureau Cedok (London) Ltd 45 Oxford Street, W1
Denmark	Danish Tourist Board 169/173 Regent Street, W1
Finland	Finnish Travel Information Centre 56 Haymarket, SW1
France	French Government Tourist Office 178 Piccadilly, W1
Germany (West)	German Tourist Information Bureau 61 Conduit Street, W1
Germany (East)	Berolina Travel Ltd 19 Dover Street, W1
Gibraltar	Gibraltar Tourist Office 15 Grand Buildings Trafalgar Square, WC2
Greece	Greek State Tourist Office 196 Regent Street, W1
Hungary	Hungarian Travel Bureau 10 Vigo Street, W1
Iceland	Iceland Tourist Information Bureau 73 Grosvenor Street, W1
Ireland (Republic)	Irish Tourist Board 150/151 New Bond Street, W1
Italy	Italian State Tourist Office 201 Regent Street, W1

Luxembourg	Luxembourg National Tourist Office
	66 Haymarket, SW1
Malta	Malta House
	Haymarket, SW1
Netherlands	Netherlands National Tourist Office
(Holland)	38 Hyde Park Gate, SW7
Norway	Norwegian National Tourist Office
	20 Pall Mall, SW1
Poland	Polish Travel Office (Orbis)
	313 Regent Street, W1
Portugal	Portuguese State Tourist Office
	20 Lower Regent Street, SW1
Rumania	Roumanian National Tourist Office
	98 Jermyn Street, SW1
Spain	Spanish National Tourist Office
	70 Jermyn Street, SW1
Sweden	Swedish National Travel Association
	52 Conduit Street, W1
Switzerland	Swiss National Tourist Office
	1 New Coventry Street, W1
Turkey	Turkish Tourism Information Office
	49 Conduit Street, W1
United Kingdom	British Tourist Authority
	Tourist Information Centre
	64 St. James's Street, SW1
U.S.S.R.	Intourist
	292 Regent Street, W1
Yugoslavia	Yugoslav National Tourist Office
	143 Regent Street, W1

General information leaflets, accommodation lists and advice may be obtained from these offices on request. They will also advise of any visa, vaccination, currency, etc., requirements in force, and provide visa application forms and the address to which they should be sent when completed.

Useful addresses and publications

British Cycling Federation
70 Brompton Road
London SW3 IEN
01-584 6706

C.T.C. Travel Ltd
13 Spring Street
London W2 3RA
01-723 8407

Cyclists' Touring Club
National Office
69 Meadrow
Godalming
Surrey GU7 3HS
Godalming 7217

English Schools Cycling Association
Secretary: G. G. Mayne
22 Quaves Lane
Bungay
Suffolk NR35 1DF
Bungay 2907

Ordre du Col Dur,
Secretary: J. R. Haigh
3 Rosehill Park West
Sutton
Surrey
01-644 8541

Rent-a-Bike Ltd
(Cycle Hire)
Kensington Student Centre
Kensington Church Street
London W8
01-937 6089

Rough Stuff Fellowship
Secretary: J. Gore
27 St. David's Road
Leyland
Preston
Lancs

Edward Stanford Ltd
(Map Specialists)
12 Long Acre
London WC2E 9LP
01-836 1321

Tandem Club
Secretary: R. J. Keane
71 Exeter Road
Welling
Kent
01-854 6482

Tricycle Association
Secretary: J. Mills
58 Townsend Avenue
West Derby
Liverpool L11 8ND

Youth Hostels Associations
England and Wales
Trevelyan House
St. Albans
Herts AL1 2DY
St. Albans 55215

Scotland
7 Glebe Crescent
Stirling
FK8 2JA
Stirling 2821

Northern Ireland
93 Dublin Road
Belfast BT2 7FE
Belfast 24733

Irish Republic
39 Mountjoy Square South
Dublin 1
Dublin 45734

PUBLICATIONS
Cycletouring: Journal of the Cyclists' Touring Club,
published every two months. Sent free to members, and
available to non-members on annual postal subscription.

Cycling: Published weekly (Wednesday). From
newsagents, or on postal subscription from I.P.C.
Specialist & Professional Press Ltd, Surrey House, Sutton,
Surrey, SM1 4QQ.

Hostelling News: Published by the Y.H.A. (England and
Wales) and sent free quarterly to all members.

Most of the other organisations and associations listed
publish their own bulletins or magazines at regular
intervals.

Metric conversion tables

Distance: 1 metre = 3·28 feet/39·37 inches
            1 kilometre = 1093·6 yards
            For practical purposes, 1 km = $\frac{5}{8}$ mile; i.e.
            8 kilometres = 5 miles, 1,000 km = 621
            miles approximately

Weight: 1 kilogram = 2 lb. 3 oz. approximately
            (2·205 lb.)

Measure: 1 litre = a little over $1\frac{3}{4}$ pints
            $4\frac{1}{2}$ litres = 1 gallon approximately

Temperature:

°F	°C
23	− 5
32	0
41	5
50	10
59	15
68	20
77	25
86	30
95	35

°C multiplied by 9, divided by 5, and 32 added to the result, gives °F.

Time differences in European countries

This table shows the number of hours *fast* which the times in other countries of Europe are on Greenwich Mean Time. Allowance must be made for British Summer Time between the dates when it is in operation.

  * Italy and Malta also advance their clocks by an hour during the summer, Italy between early June and the end of September, Malta between mid-June and early September. Ireland changes to Summer Time between the same dates as the U.K.

Country	Hours fast on G.M.T.	
	winter	summer
Austria	1	1
Belgium	1	1
Bulgaria	2	2
Cyprus	2	2
Czechoslovakia	1	1
Denmark	1	1
Finland	2	2
France	1	1
Germany	1	1
Gibraltar	1	1
Greece	2	2
Hungary	1	1
Iceland	–	–
Ireland*	–	1
Italy*	1	2
Luxembourg	1	1
Malta*	1	2

Netherlands	1	1
Norway	1	1
Poland	1	1
Portugal	1	1
Rumania	2	2
Spain	1	1
Sweden	1	1
Switzerland	1	1
Turkey	2	2
United Kingdom	–	1
U.S.S.R. (Moscow)	3	3
Yugoslavia	1	1

Units of currency

Austria	Schilling (= 100 groschen)
Belgium	Franc (= 100 centimes)
Bulgaria	Lev (= 100 stotinki)
Cyprus	Cyprus Pound (= 1,000 mils)
Czechoslovakia	Crown (= 100 heller)
Denmark	Krone (= 100 øre)
Finland	Markka (Mark) (= 100 pennia)
France	Franc (= 100 centimes)
W. Germany	Mark (= 100 pfennig)
E. Germany	Mark der Deutschen Notenbank (= 100 pfennig)
Gibraltar	Gibraltar Pound (= 100 pence)
Greece	Drachma (= 100 lepta)
Hungary	Florint (= 100 filler)
Iceland	Krona (= 100 aurars)
Irish Republic	Pound (= 100 pence)
Italy	Lira
Luxembourg	Franc (= 100 centimes)
Malta	Malta Pound (= 100 cents)
Netherlands	Gulden (Guilder) or Florin (= 100 cents)
Norway	Krone (= 100 øre)
Poland	Zloty (= 100 groszy)
Portugal	Escudo (= 100 centavos)
Rumania	Leu (= 100 bani)
Spain	Peseta (= 100 centimos)
Sweden	Krona (= 100 öre)
Switzerland	Franc (= 100 centimes, or rappen)
Turkey	Turkish Pound (Liras) (= 100 kurus)
United Kingdom	Pound (= 100 pence)
U.S.S.R.	Rouble (= 100 kopecs)
Yugoslavia	Dinar (= 100 paras)

Average monthly temperatures of selected European towns

Place	Height above Sea Level (ft./m.)	Annual Rainfall (ins./mm.)	Jan.	Feb.	Mar.	Apr.	May	June	July	Aug.	Sept.	Oct.	Nov.	Dec.
Ajaccio	243/74	29/739	56/13	58/14	62/17	66/19	72/22	79/26	85/29	85/29	81/27	72/22	64/18	59/15
Amsterdam	5/2	26/650	40/4	41/5	46/8	52/11	60/16	65/18	69/21	68/20	64/18	56/13	47/8	41/5
Athens	351/107	15/384	54/12	55/13	60/16	67/19	77/25	85/29	90/32	90/32	83/28	74/23	64/18	57/14
Barcelona	312/95	24/597	56/13	57/14	61/16	64/18	71/22	77/25	81/27	82/28	78/26	71/22	62/17	57/14
Belgrade	453/138	25/625	37/3	41/5	53/12	64/18	74/23	79/26	84/29	83/28	76/24	65/18	52/11	40/4
Bergen	141/43	79/2001	43/6	44/7	47/8	55/13	64/18	70/21	72/22	70/21	64/18	57/14	49/9	45/7
Biarritz	112/34	49/1225	52/11	54/12	57/14	60/16	66/19	71/22	74/23	76/24	73/23	67/19	58/14	54/12
Brussels	328/100	33/838	42/6	43/6	49/9	56/13	65/18	70/21	73/23	72/22	67/19	58/14	47/8	42/6
Cagliari	5/2	15/381	57/14	58/14	62/17	65/18	72/22	80/27	86/30	85/29	80/27	74/23	66/19	62/17
Clermont-Ferrand	1322/403	24/622	44/7	48/9	54/12	60/16	68/20	74/23	78/26	78/26	73/23	63/17	52/11	46/8
Cologne	184/56	27/696	40/4	43/6	49/9	57/14	66/19	71/22	73/23	72/22	66/19	57/14	47/8	42/6
Como	738/225	50/1280	43/6	51/11	54/12	64/18	71/22	81/27	85/29	82/28	77/25	64/18	53/12	46/8
Constanta	13/4	15/384	37/3	41/5	46/8	55/13	66/19	75/24	79/26	79/26	72/22	62/17	51/11	43/6
Copenhagen	43/13	23/592	36/2	41/5	50/10	61/16	67/19	72/22	69/21	63/17	53/12	53/12	43/6	38/3
Dublin	155/47	30/754	47/8	47/8	51/11	54/12	59/15	65/18	69/21	67/19	63/17	57/14	51/11	47/8
Dubrovnik	59/18	56/1435	50/10	51/11	54/12	63/17	70/21	76/24	80/27	79/26	72/22	69/21	60/16	52/11
Edinburgh	441/134	28/701	43/6	43/6	47/8	50/10	55/13	62/17	65/18	64/18	60/16	53/12	47/8	44/7
Florence	121/37	36/919	49/9	53/12	60/16	68/20	75/24	84/29	89/32	88/31	81/27	69/21	58/14	50/10
Geneva	1329/405	34/861	39/4	43/6	53/12	60/16	66/19	73/23	77/25	76/24	69/21	58/14	47/8	40/4
Hamburg	86/26	29/734	35/2	37/3	42/6	51/11	60/16	67/19	69/21	67/19	63/17	53/12	44/7	38/3
Helsinki	30/9	28/700	27/−3	26/−3	32/0	43/6	55/13	63/17	71/22	66/19	57/14	45/7	37/3	31/−1
Innsbruck	1909/582	34/859	34/1	40/4	51/11	60/16	69/21	78/26	78/26	76/24	69/21	58/14	46/8	36/2
Istanbul	59/18	32/800	45/7	47/8	52/11	61/16	68/20	77/25	81/27	81/27	75/24	67/19	59/18	51/11
Klagenfurt	1471/448	38/973	29/−2	37/3	48/9	59/15	67/19	74/23	77/25	75/24	68/20	56/13	42/6	33/1
Leghorn	20/6	23/594	52/11	54/12	57/14	62/17	69/21	75/24	80/27	80/27	76/24	69/21	61/16	55/13

Average Temperature at 1400 hrs. (°F./°C.)

Place	Height above Sea Level (ft./m.)	Annual Rainfall (ins./mm.)	Average Temperature at 1400 hrs. (°F./°C.)											
			Jan.	Feb.	Mar.	Apr.	May	June	July	Aug.	Sept.	Oct.	Nov.	Dec.
Lisbon	313/95	27/686	56/13	58/14	61/16	64/18	69/21	75/24	79/26	80/27	76/24	69/21	62/17	57/14
London	18/5	24/605	43/6	45/7	49/9	55/13	62/17	68/20	71/22	70/21	65/18	56/13	49/9	45/7
Lucerne	1476/450	46/1178	32/0	45/7	49/9	53/12	61/16	68/20	71/22	69/21	63/17	52/11	43/6	35/2
Luxembourg	1096/334	29/742	36/2	40/4	49/9	58/15	65/18	71/22	74/23	73/23	65/18	56/13	45/7	39/4
Madrid	2188/667	17/419	47/8	51/11	57/14	64/18	71/22	80/27	87/31	86/30	77/25	66/19	54/12	48/9
Malaga	108/33	18/447	61/16	62/17	64/18	69/21	74/23	80/27	84/29	85/29	81/27	74/23	67/19	62/17
Milan	341/103	32/803	40/4	47/8	56/13	66/19	72/22	80/27	84/29	82/28	76/24	64/18	51/11	42/6
Munich	1739/530	34/866	33/1	37/3	45/7	54/12	63/17	69/21	72/12	71/22	64/18	53/12	42/6	36/2
Naples	220/67	34/871	54/12	55/13	60/16	67/19	73/23	81/27	86/30	86/30	81/27	72/22	63/17	57/14
Nice	39/12	32/820	56/13	56/13	59/15	64/18	69/21	76/24	81/27	82/28	81/27	72/22	62/17	58/14
Nicosia	716/218	14/363	58/14	59/15	65/18	74/23	80/28	91/33	97/36	91/33	81/27	81/27	72/22	62/17
Oslo	308/94	27/683	30/−1	32/0	40/4	50/10	62/17	69/21	73/23	69/21	60/16	49/9	37/3	31/−1
Palermo	354/108	28/709	58/14	60/16	62/17	67/19	83/28	82/28	86/30	87/31	83/28	75/24	67/19	61/16
Paris	164/50	22/566	42/6	45/7	52/11	60/16	57/19	73/23	76/24	73/23	65/18	59/15	49/9	43/6
Prague	682/208	19/490	34/1	38/3	39/4	43/6	50/10	55/13	58/14	57/14	51/11	44/7	39/4	34/1
Rejkjavik	92/28	34/861	36/2	37/3	39/4	43/6	50/10	55/13	58/14	57/14	51/11	44/7	39/4	38/3
Rijeka	16/5	62/1575	47/8	55/13	55/13	62/17	71/22	77/25	83/28	83/28	75/24	65/18	56/13	51/11
Rome	377/115	26/653	54/12	56/13	62/17	68/20	74/23	82/28	88/31	88/31	83/28	73/23	63/17	56/13
St. Malo	23/7	22/556	48/9	50/10	53/12	57/14	63/17	67/19	71/22	71/22	68/20	60/16	53/12	50/10
Sofia	1805/550	25/635	34/1	39/4	51/11	62/17	70/21	76/24	82/28	82/28	74/23	63/17	50/10	37/3
Stockholm	146/46	22/569	31/−1	31/−1	37/3	45/7	57/14	65/18	70/21	66/19	58/14	48/9	38/3	33/1
Tromsø	335/108	40/1019	30/−1	29/−2	32/0	37/3	44/7	53/12	59/15	57/14	49/9	40/4	34/1	31/−1
Venice	13/4	29/726	43/6	46/8	54/12	63/17	71/22	78/26	82/28	82/28	78/26	65/18	54/12	46/8
Vienna	664/202	26/650	34/1	38/3	47/8	57/14	66/19	71/22	75/24	73/23	66/19	55/13	44/7	37/3
Warsaw	394/120	22/559	30/−1	32/0	41/5	54/12	67/19	72/22	75/24	73/23	65/18	54/12	40/4	32/0

Index

Accommodation 70–73, 90, 91
Albania 195
Andorra 122
Austria 94–96
Bags for Cycles 56–60
Belgium 96–100
Berlin 129
Bottom Bracket 18
Brakes 23
Bulgaria 100–103
Camping 75–81
Carriage of Cycles 42–45,
 89–90
Chain 25
Checking the Cycle 40, 41
Children 32–37
Clothing 47–53
Cranks 19
Currency 84–86, 248
Customs 86
Cyclists' Touring Club 46, 67,
 81, 224
Cyprus 103–105
Czechoslovakia 105–107
Denmark 107–110
Distance 67
England 177–183
Equipment Lists 237–239
Family Cycling 32–37
Finland 110–112
Food 68–69
Frames 15, 18

France 113–122
Gears 25–28
Germany (East) 122–124
Germany (West) 125–130
Gibraltar 166
Gozo 147
Greece 130–132
Handlebars 19, 20
Health 69, 86, 87
Holland 148–151
Hubs 24
Hungary 132–134
Iceland 135–138
Inner Tubes 24
Insurance 46
Ireland (Republic) 139–142
Ireland (Northern) 188–190
Italy 142–146
Ladies 37
Language 87–89
Liechtenstein 174
Lighting 28
Luxembourg 96–100
Malta 147
Maps 61–66
Metric Conversion Tables 245
Monaco 122
Mudguards 24
Netherlands 148–151
Norway 151–156
Pass Climbing 89, 90
Passports 82–83

Pedals 19
Poland 156–158
Portugal 158–160
Publications 244
Pyrenees 204–213
Riding Style 29
'Rough Stuff' 91
Rumania 160–162
Saddles 22
San Marino 146
Scotland 183–186, 196–204
Sleeping Bags 78–79
Somerset 213–221
Spain 162–166
Spares 53–55, 89
Stoves 79–80
Suggested Tours:
    Austria/Germany 233–236
    Cotswolds 225–226
    France 232–233
    Norfolk/Suffolk 228–230
    Wales 226–228
    Wessex 223–225

Yorkshire 230–232
Sweden 166–169
Switzerland 169–173
Tandems 30
Temperatures 249–250
Tents 75–78
Time Differences 246–247
Tools 53–55
Towpath Riding 91, 92
Tourist Offices 240–241
Training 38, 39
Tricycles 31, 32
Turkey-in-Europe 174–176
Tyres 24
U.S.S.R. 195
Useful Addresses 242–244
Vatican City State 147
Visas 83–84
Wales 186–188
Wheels 23
Youth Hostels 72–73
Yugoslavia 190–195